500 Cross-Stitch Blocks

Anna Davidson

Sterling Publishing Co., Inc. New York
A Sterling/Chapelle Book

Chapelle Ltd.

Owner: Jo Packham

Editor: Karmen Quinney

Graphics Coordinator: Susan Jorgensen

Staff: Areta Bingham, Kass Burchett, Jill Dahlberg,
Marilyn Goff, Holly Hollingsworth,
Barbara Milburn, Linda Orton, Cindy Stoeckl,
Kim Taylor, Sara Toliver, Kristi Torsak,
Desirée Wybrow

Photography: Kevin Dilley/Hazen Photo Studio

We would like to offer our sincere appreciation
for the valuable support given in this ever-
changing industry of new ideas, concepts,
designs, and products. Several projects shown
in this publication were created with outstand-
ing and innovative products developed by Caron
Collection, DMC, Mill Hill Beads, and Zweigart
Fabric.

Library of Congress Cataloging-in-Publication Data

Davidson, Anna.
   500 cross-stitch blocks / Anna Davidson
     p. cm.
   Includes index.
   ISBN 0-8069-7143-6
    1. Cross-stitch–Patterns. I. Title: Cross-stitch blocks. II. Title.
  TT778.C76 .D35 2001
  746.44'3041–dc21

                      2001040095

10 9 8 7 6 5 4 3 2 1

Published by Sterling Publishing Company, Inc.,
387 Park Avenue South, New York, NY 10016
© 2001 by Anna Davidson
Distributed in Canada by Sterling Publishing
⅟ Canadian Manda Group, One Atlantic Avenue, Suite 105
Toronto, Ontario, Canada M6K 3E7
Distributed in Great Britain and Europe by Cassell PLC
Wellington House, 125 Strand, London WC2R 0BB, England
Distributed in Australia by Capricorn Link (Australia) Pty Ltd.
P.O. Box 704, Windsor, NSW 2756, Australia
Printed in China
All Rights Reserved

Sterling ISBN 0-8069-7143-6

If you have any questions or comments, please
contact: Chapelle Ltd., Inc.,
P.O. Box 9252 Ogden, UT 84409
(801) 621-2777 • FAX (801) 621-2788 •
e-mail: chapelle@ chapelleltd.com •
website: www.chapelleltd.com

About the Author

Anna Davidson lives in Half Moon Bay, California, with her husband Nicholas and their two children, Alistair, 13, and Zoë, 10. She arrived in the United States from Britain thirteen years ago with her husband and ten week old son. In her luggage along with diapers and bottles were embroidery flosses and 14 hpi Aida fabric. She had fallen in love with the colorful simplicity of cross-stitch a few months before her departure from Britain. All through the lonely months of settling in a foreign country, her embroidery was a great source of comfort and a wonderful outlet for creativity. The difficulty of finding cross-stitch designs that she wanted to stitch spurred Anna into designing her own pieces.

Anna feels that cross-stitch is kind to the learner. It is a basic stitch, easily formed on fabric designed for the purpose. Its simplicity also means that it is a perfect introduction to stitching for children—Anna teaches cross-stitch in her daughter's school. In addition, Anna feels that cross-stitch is also kind to the beginning designer. With squared paper, colored pencils, and perseverance, designs of her own appeared on the fabric at her fingertips. She has achieved a finalist's place in two DMC competitions and has had her work featured regularly in British stitching magazines.

Acknowledgments

I would like to thank Dover Publications for their permission to use their beautifully illustrated books as spurs to my own imagination. One book in particular has been an inspiration to me, *Art Nouveau Animal Designs and Patterns* by M.P. Verneuil 1992. I would also like to thank Susan and Michael Bryant, who encouraged me to teach in their wonderful needle-work store The Status Thimble, in Burlingame, California. Their photographs of tiles of Medieval Europe were invaluable—without these, the pages of this book would not be so varied.

Dedication

This book is dedicated to Nicholas, Alistair, and Zoë, my loving family.

Contents

Pages 56–57 Catalina Floral

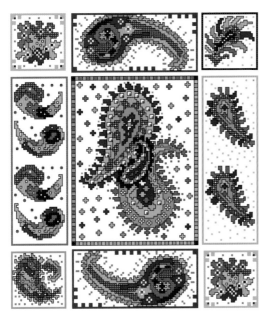

Pages 94–95 Outragious Paisley

Pages 118–119 Sunlight in the Garden

Introduction

Contained in this book are over 500 cross-stitch designs. Each double-page spread of graphed designs is made up of borders, small motifs, and large motifs that can be made to fit together like tiles on a wall or quilt blocks. One color code has been provided for each double-page spread. The cross-stitch designs can also be combined with other motifs from other pages to create a different and unique look to the piece you are stitching. A piece could be combined to tell a story, border another stitched piece, or stand on its own as a single motif. The borders can be placed in the middle of a block to break up a large expanse of fabric.

At times it may be necessary to adjust the stitching to fit the piece that you are trying to make. The ends of continuing or extended pieces have been left open to match up with the pattern. Use your imagination and creativity to come up with ways to make these patterns work for your individual taste. It is suggested that copies be made of the patterns, cut, then pasted to graph paper, allowing you to see how the pattern will fit together and to make necessary adjustments on the paper before beginning to stitch. This book has included several combinations of pieces called block samples. Block samples can be seen on pages 4, 7, 126, and 127.

Cross-stitch Items to Know

Fabric for Cross-stitch

Counted cross-stitch is worked on even-weave fabrics. These fabrics are manufactured specifically for counted-thread embroidery, and are woven with the same number of vertical as horizontal threads per inch.

Because the number of threads in the fabric is equal in each direction, each stitch will be the same size. The number of threads per inch in even-weave fabrics determines the size of a finished design.

Number of Strands

The number of strands used per stitch varies, depending on the fabric used. Generally, the rule to follow for cross-stitching is three strands on Aida 11, two strands on Aida 14, one or two strands on Aida 18 (depending on desired thickness of stitches), and one strand on Hardanger 22.

For backstitching, use one strand on all fabrics. When completing a French Knot (FK), use two strands and one wrap on all fabrics, unless otherwise directed.

Finished Design Size

To determine the size of the finished design, divide the stitch count by the number of threads per inch of fabric. When a design is stitched over two threads, divide stitch count by half the threads per inch. For example, if a design with a stitch count of 120 width and 250 height was stitched on a 28 count linen (over two threads making it 14 count), the finished size would be 8⅝" x 17⅞".

$$120 \div 14" = 8\tfrac{5}{8}" \text{ (width)}$$

$$250 \div 14" = 17\tfrac{7}{8}" \text{ (height)}$$

$$\text{Finished size} = 8\tfrac{5}{8}" \text{ x } 17\tfrac{7}{8}"$$

Preparing Fabric

Cut fabric at least 3" larger on all sides than the finished design size to ensure enough space for desired assembly. To prevent fraying, whipstitch or machine-zigzag along the raw edges or apply liquid fray preventive.

Needles for Cross-stitch

Blunt needles should slip easily through the fabric holes without piercing fabric threads. For fabric with 11 or fewer threads per inch, use a tapestry needle #24; for 14 threads per inch, use a tapestry needle #24, #26, or #28; for 18 or more threads per inch, use a tapestry needle #26 or #28. Avoid leaving the needle in the design area of the fabric. It may leave rust or a permanent impression on the fabric.

Floss

All numbers and color names on the codes represent the DMC brand of floss. Use 18" lengths of floss. For best coverage, separate the strands and dampen with a wet sponge, then put together the number of strands required for the fabric used.

Centering Design on Fabric

Fold the fabric in half horizontally, then vertically. Place a pin in the intersection to mark the center. Locate the center of the design on the graph. Begin stitching all designs at the center point of the graph and fabric. Dots have been placed next to each motif to aid in locating the center of the design.

Securing Floss

Insert needle up from the underside of the fabric at starting point. Hold 1" of thread behind the fabric and stitch over it, securing with the first few stitches. To finish thread, run under four or more stitches on the back

of the design. Avoid knotting floss, unless working on clothing.

Another method of securing floss is the waste knot. Knot floss and insert needle down from the right top side of the fabric about 1" from design area. Work several stitches over the thread to secure. Cut off the knot later.

Carrying Floss

To carry floss, run floss under the previously worked stitches on the back. Do not carry thread across any fabric that is not or will not be stitched. Loose threads, especially dark ones, will show through the fabric.

Cleaning Finished Design

When stitching is finished, soak the fabric in cold water with a mild soap for five to ten minutes. Rinse well and roll in a towel to remove excess water. Do not wring. Place the piece face down on a dry towel and iron on a warm setting until the fabric is dry.

Stitching Techniques

Backstitch (BS)

1. Insert needle up between woven threads at A.

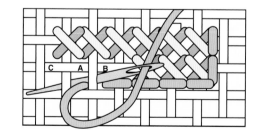

2. Go down at B, one opening to the right.

3. Come up at C.

4. Go down at A, one opening to the right.

Bead Attachment (BD)

Beads should sit facing the same direction as the top cross-stitch.

1. Make first half of cross-stitch.

2. Insert needle up between woven threads at A.

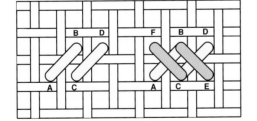

3. Thread on bead before going down at B, the opening diagonally across from A.

4. To strengthen stitch, come up again at A and either go through bead again or if the thread is doubled, split threads to lay around bead and go down at B again.

Cross-stitch (XS)

Stitches are done in a row or, if necessary, one at a time in an area.

1. Insert needle up between woven threads at A.

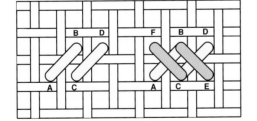

2. Go down at B, the opening diagonally across from A.

3. Come up at C and go down at D, etc.

4. To complete the top stitches creating an "X", come up at E and go down at B, come up at C and go down at F, etc. All top stitches should lie in the same direction.

French Knot (FK)

1. Insert needle up between woven threads at A, using one strand of embroidery floss.

2. Loosely wrap floss once around needle.

3. Go down at B, the opening across from A. Pull floss taut as needle is pushed down through fabric.

4. Carry floss across back of work between knots.

Tent Stitch (TS)

1. Insert needle up between woven threads at A.

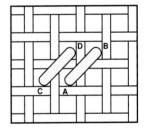

2. Go down at B, the opening diagonally across from A.

3. Come up at C and go down at D, working right to left. The stitch should go the same direction as the top stitch of the cross-stitch.

A Sense of Place

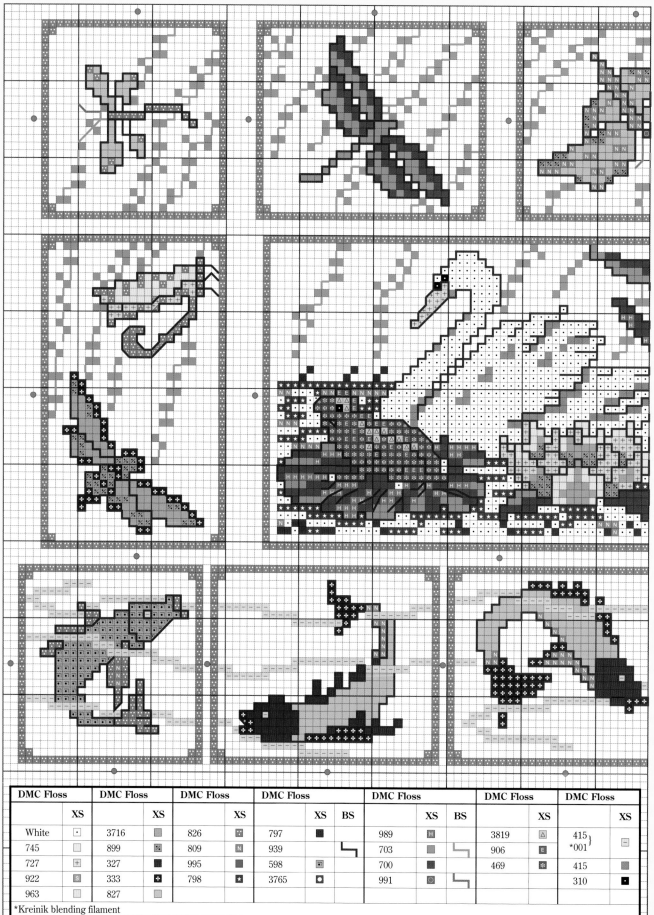

DMC Floss		DMC Floss		DMC Floss		DMC Floss			DMC Floss			DMC Floss		DMC Floss	
	XS		XS		XS		XS	BS		XS	BS		XS		XS
White	·	3716		826		797	■		989	H		3819	△	415 }	
745		899		809	N	939			703			906	E	*001 }	⊟
727	+	327	■	995		598	⊡		700	■		469	✳	415	
922	S	333	✚	798	✦	3765	◉		991	◎				310	▪
963		827													

*Kreinik blending filament

Motifs designed to be
stitched on white fabric.

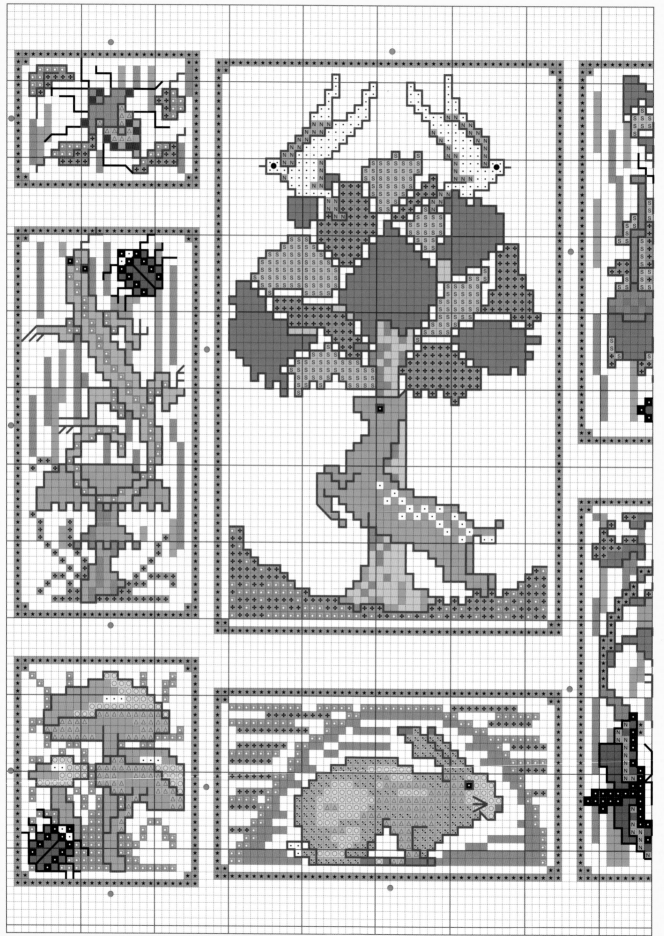

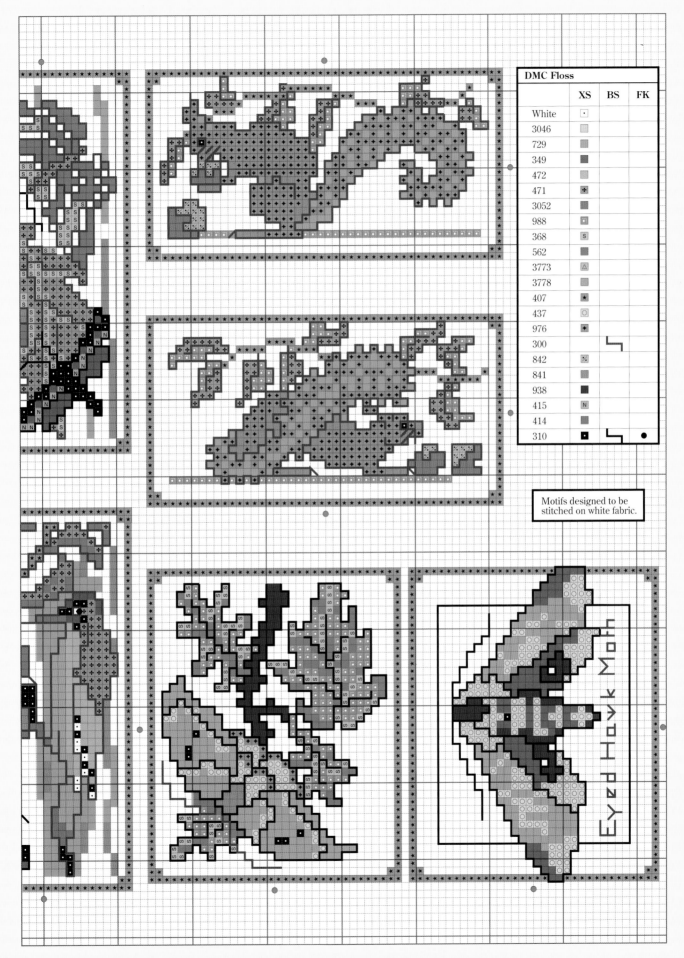

DMC Floss			
	XS	BS	FK
White	·		
3046			
729			
349			
472			
471	+		
3052			
988	·		
368	S		
562			
3773	△		
3778			
407	★		
437	○		
976	+		
300		⌐	
842	∴		
841			
938			
415	N		
414			
310	·	⌐	●

Motifs designed to be
stitched on white fabric.

Eyed Hawk Moth

See page 126 for complete verse.

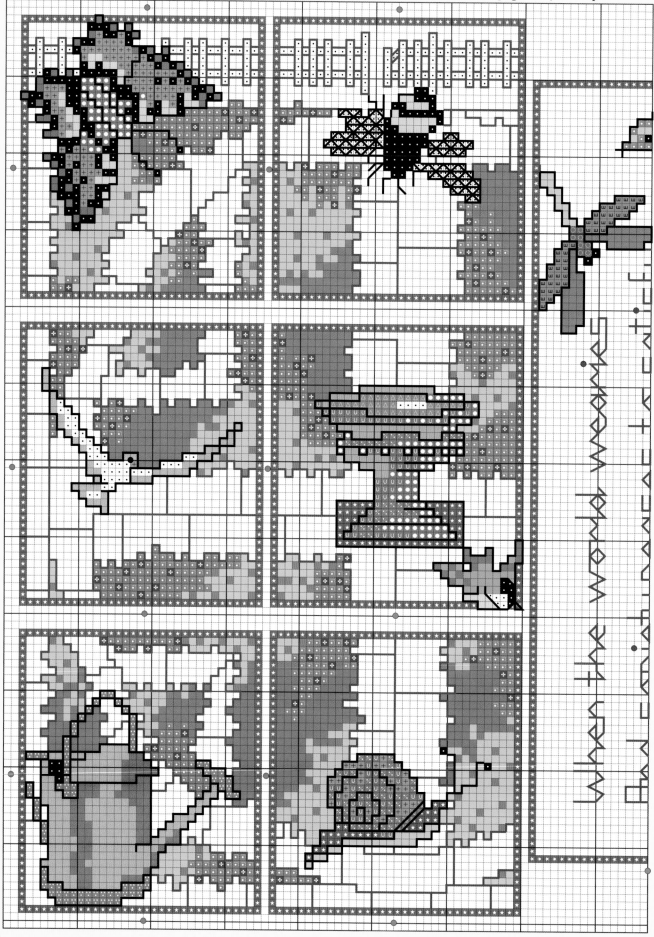

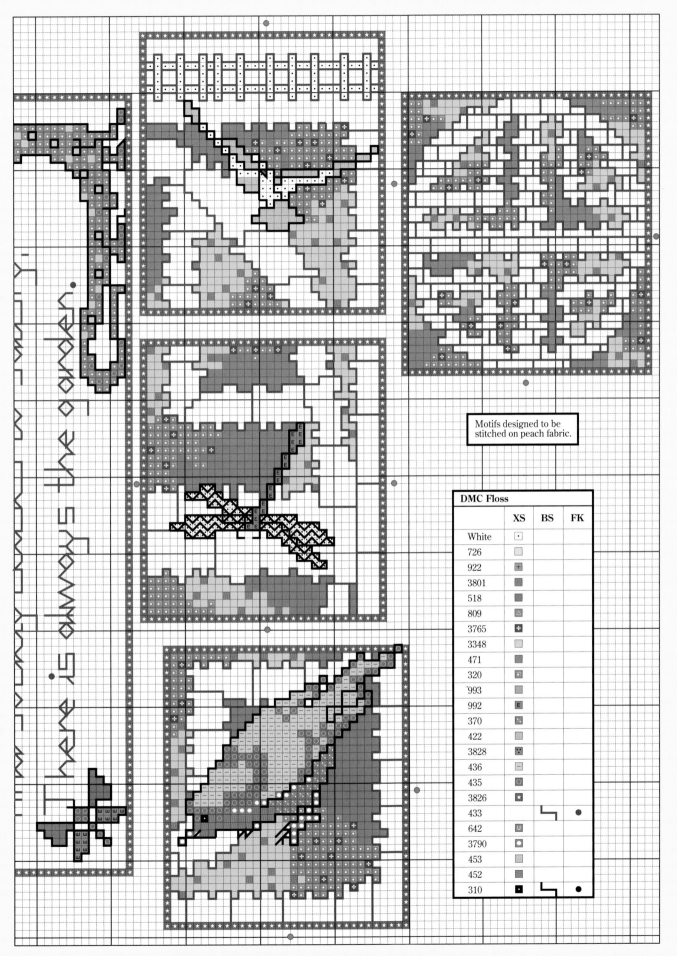

Motifs designed to be
stitched on peach fabric.

DMC Floss			
	XS	BS	FK
White	·		
726			
922	+		
3801			
518			
809	△		
3765	+		
3348			
471			
320			
993			
992	E		
370			
422			
3828			
436	−		
435	⊘		
3826	✦		
433		⌐	●
642	U		
3790	⊙		
453			
452			
310	■	⌐	●

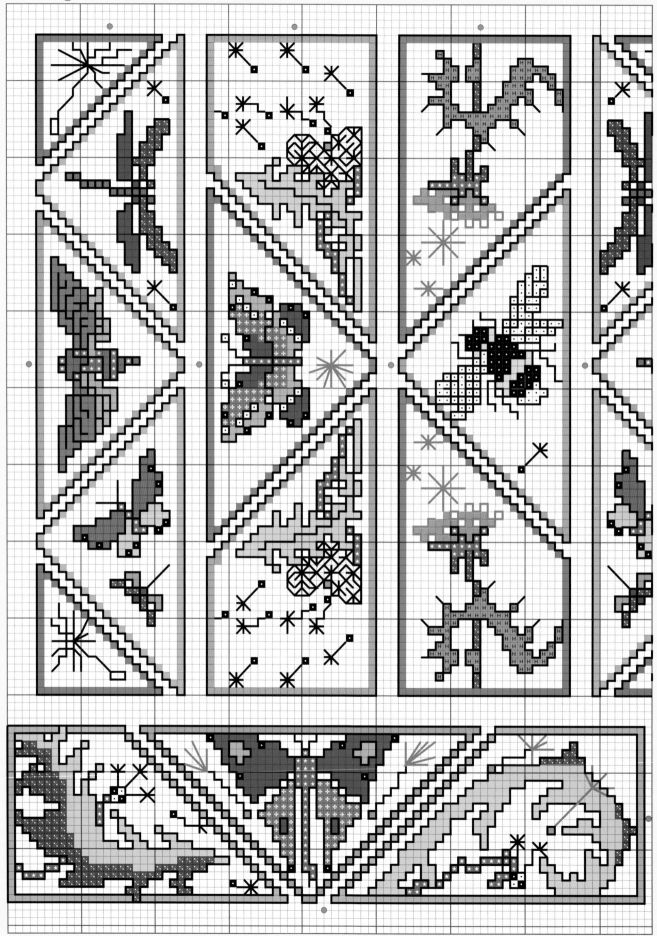

Motifs designed to be stitched on cream fabric.

DMC Floss		
	XS	BS
White	·	
744		
922		
900		
3041		
3685		
3755		
322		
798		
3348		
895		⌐
502	H	
958		
434		
648		
414		⌐
310	·	⌐

17

DMC Floss		DMC Floss		DMC Floss		DMC Floss			DMC Floss			DMC Floss		
	XS		XS		XS		XS	BS		XS	BS		XS	BS
White	·	321	■	3819	▨	989	■	⌐	928	▨	⌐	918	✦	⌐
677	☐	498	▣	368	▨	987	✛		3826	◉		310	▪	
725	▨													

Motifs designed to be stitched on oatmeal fabric.

19

See page 126 for complete verse.

A church of silent weathered
A breezy reddish tower
A yard whose mounded restin
Are tinged with sorrel flower

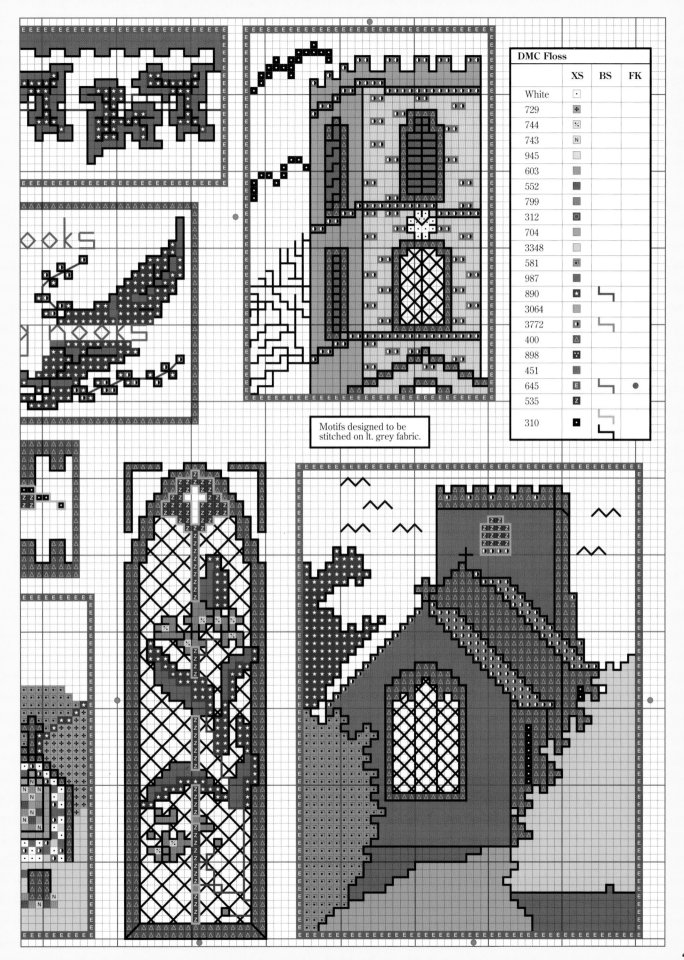

Motifs designed to be
stitched on lt. grey fabric.

DMC Floss			
	XS	BS	FK
White	·		
729	✦		
744	▨		
743	N		
945			
603			
552			
799			
312	◉		
704			
3348			
581	▣		
987			
890	★	⌐	
3064			
3772	▯	⌐	
400	△		
898	▦		
451			
645	E	⌐	●
535	Z		
310	■	⌐	

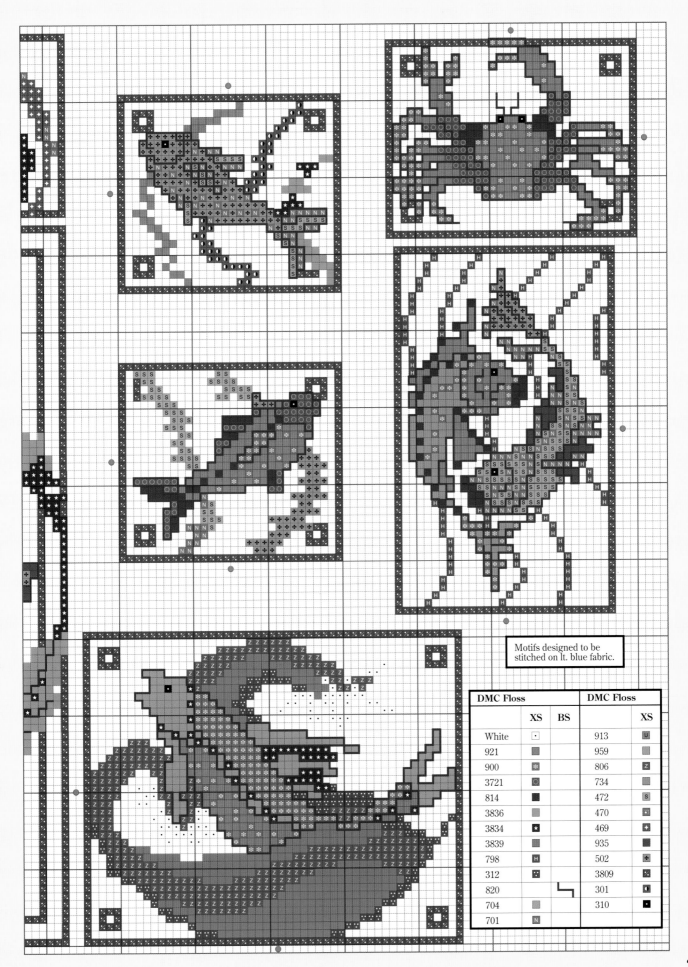

Motifs designed to be
stitched on lt. blue fabric.

DMC Floss			DMC Floss	
	XS	BS		XS
White	·		913	U
921	▨		959	▨
900	✳		806	Z
3721	◉		734	▨
814	■		472	S
3836	▨		470	⊡
3834	★		469	✚
3839	▨		935	■
798	H		502	✚
312	✳		3809	✳
820		⌐	301	◐
704	▨		310	■
701	N			

Motifs designed to be stitched on black fabric.

DMC Floss			DMC Floss			DMC Floss	
	XS	BS		XS	BS		XS
3852	▨	⌐	372		⌐	435	▣
221	■		976	◑		400	✦

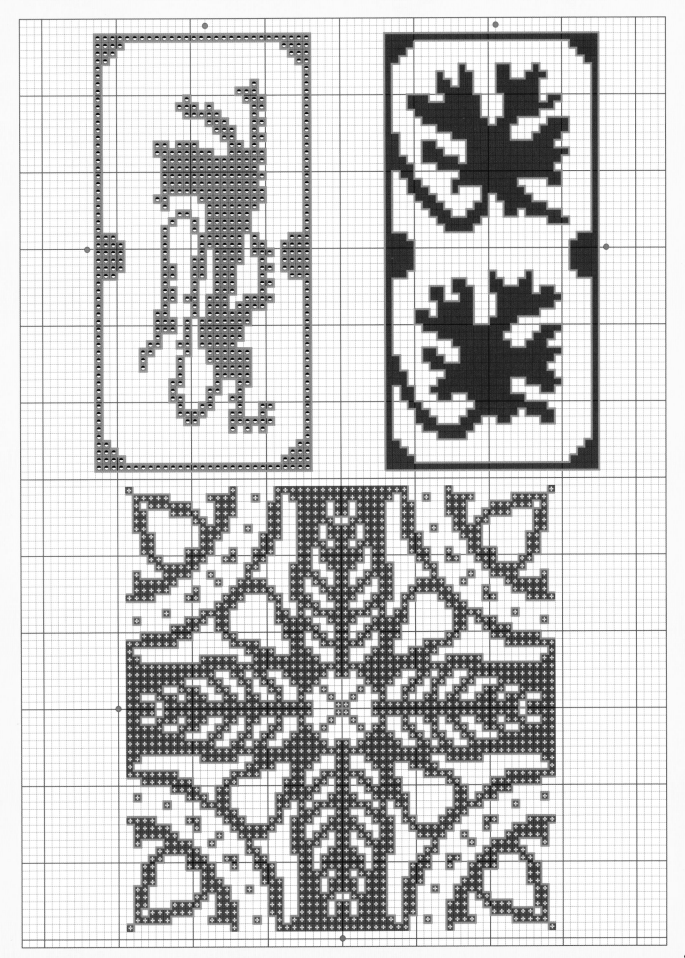

25

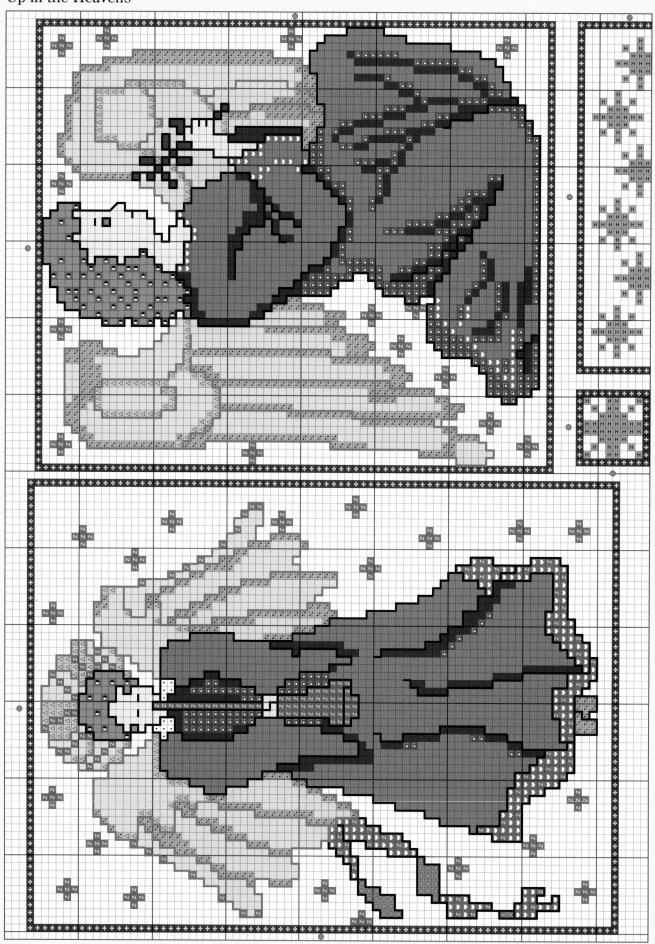

Motifs designed to be
stitched on dk. blue fabric.

DMC Floss

	XS	BS	BD
White	·		
726			
3820			
972	△		
5282	Z	⌐	
948			
498			
996	◉		
5290	♥		
3839			
798	▪		
820			
939	✠		
3345			
976			
434			
300			
310		⌐	
02002			+
02011			H

Motifs designed to be
stitched on lt. blue fabric.

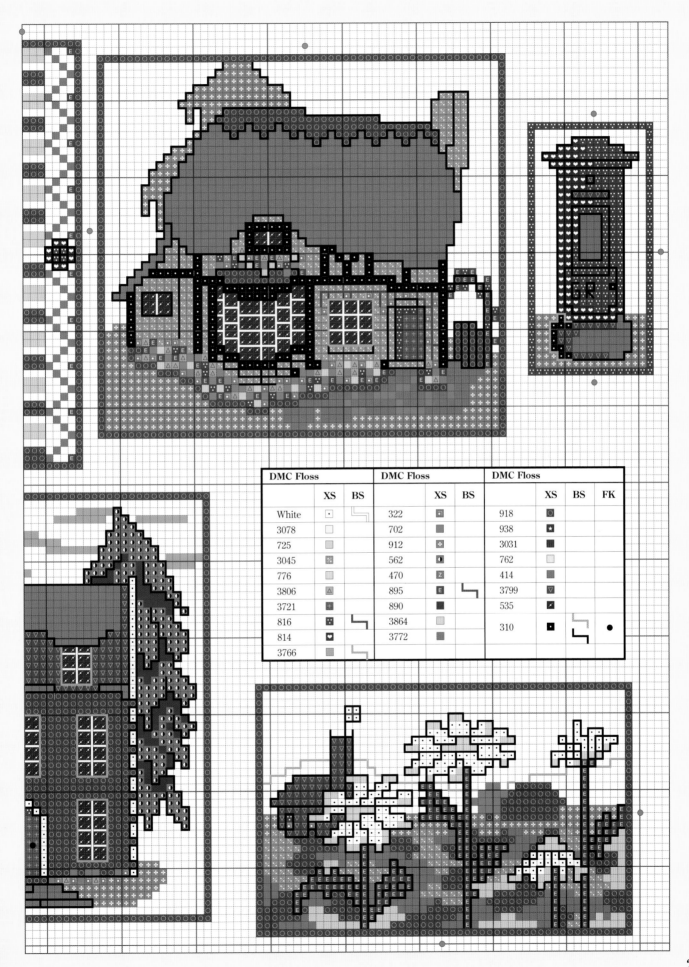

DMC Floss			DMC Floss			DMC Floss			
	XS	BS		XS	BS		XS	BS	FK
White			322			918			
3078			702			938			
725			912			3031			
3045			562			762			
776			470			414			
3806			895			3799			
3721			890			535			
816			3864			310			
814			3772						
3766									

a *World* of *Florals*

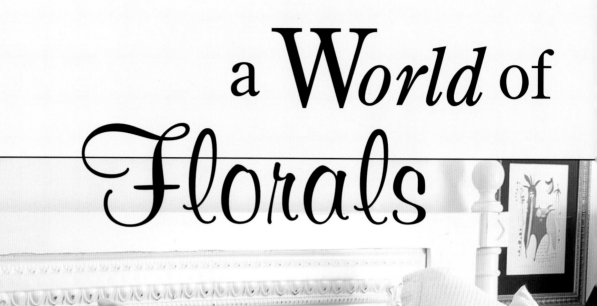

31

Motifs designed to be stitched on white fabric.

DMC Floss	XS	BS
727		
726		
725		
741		
781		
813		
799		
825		
792		
820		
704		
3347		
912	E	
3812		
3818		

Medieval Floral

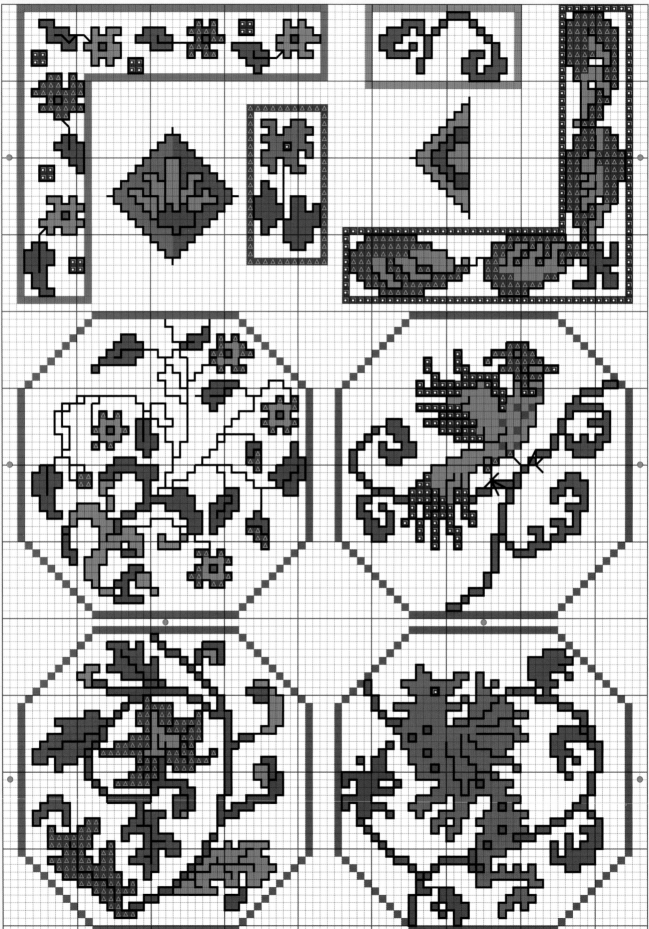

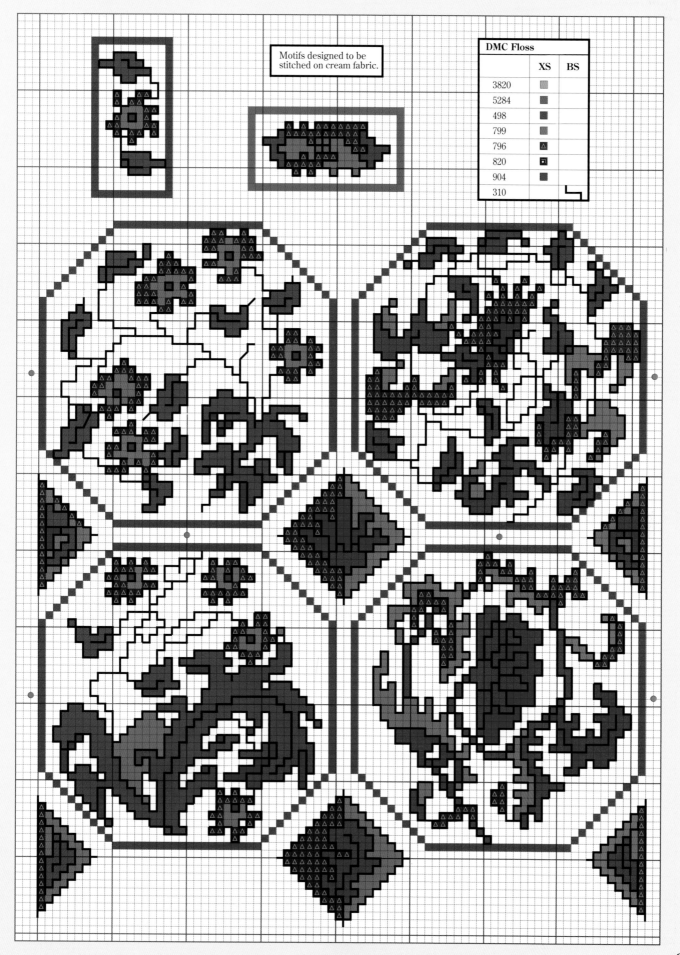

Motifs designed to be
stitched on cream fabric.

DMC Floss		
	XS	BS
3820		
5284		
498		
799		
796		
820		
904		
310		

Indian Floral

Motifs designed to be
stitched on dirty linen fabric.

DMC Floss		
	XS	**BS**
White	·	
743		
742		
351		
3328		
816		
794		
820		
989		
501	★	
310		

37

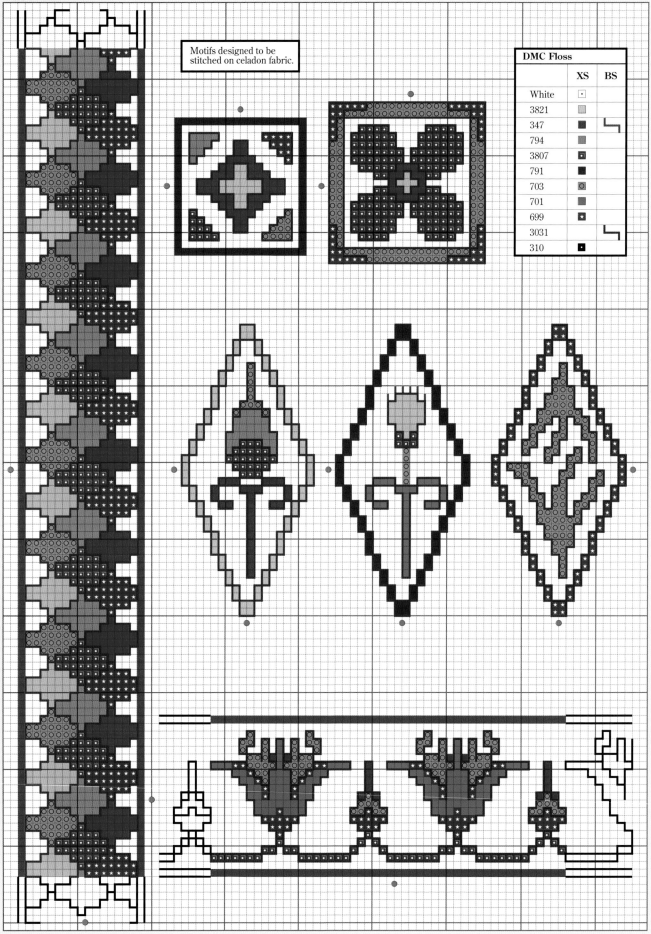

Motifs designed to be stitched on celadon fabric.

DMC Floss		
	XS	BS
White	·	
3821		
347		⌐
794		
3807	·	
791		
703	◉	
701		
699	✶	
3031		⌐
310	▪	

DMC Floss			
	XS	BS	FK
738			
3064			
400			
839			

Motifs designed to be
stitched on rue green fabric.

Alphabet Floral

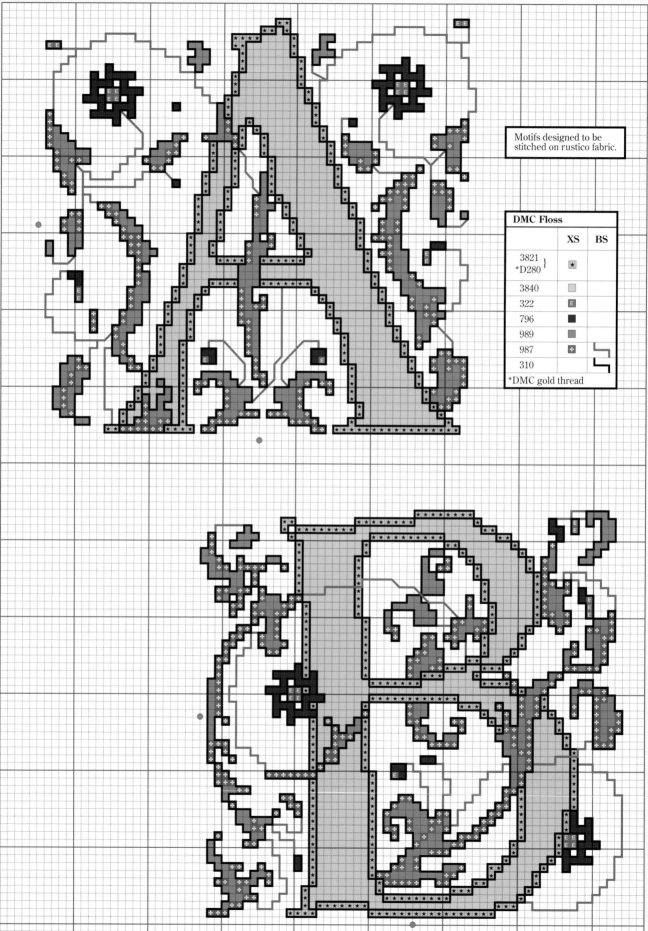

Motifs designed to be
stitched on rustico fabric.

DMC Floss		
	XS	BS
3821 } *D280	★	
3840		
322	E	
796		
989		
987	✛	
310		
*DMC gold thread		

43

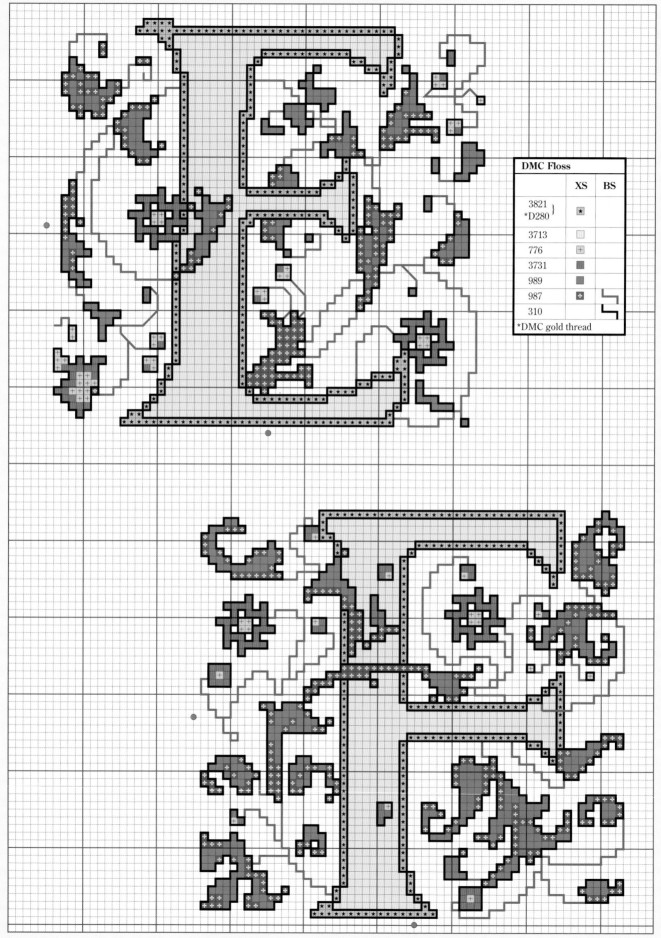

DMC Floss		
	XS	BS
3821 } *D280	★	
3713		
776	+	
3731		
989		
987	+	
310		
*DMC gold thread		

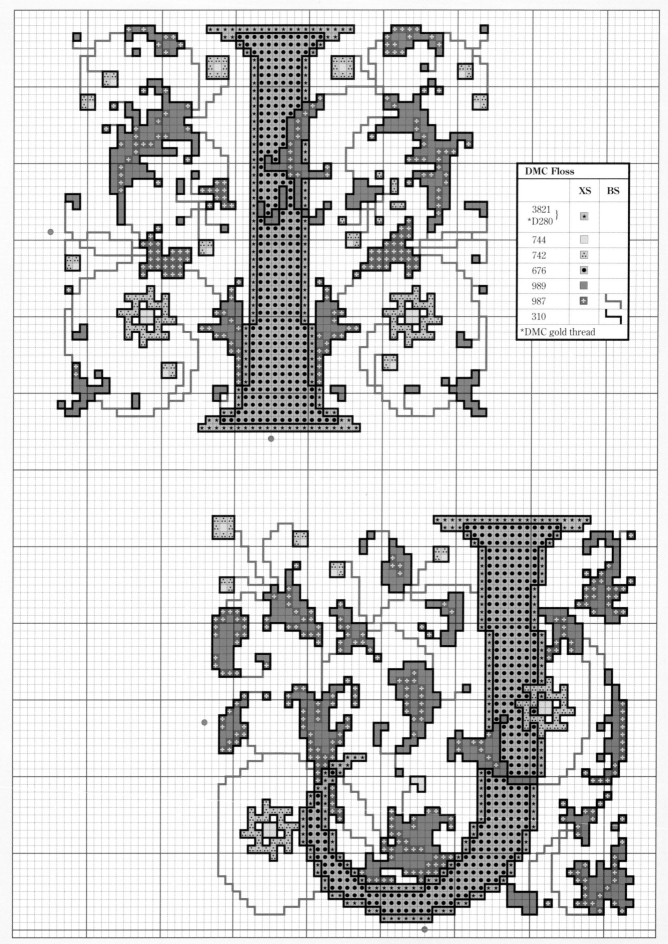

DMC Floss		
	XS	BS
3821 } *D280	★	
744		
742		
676	●	
989		
987	✤	
310		
*DMC gold thread		

46

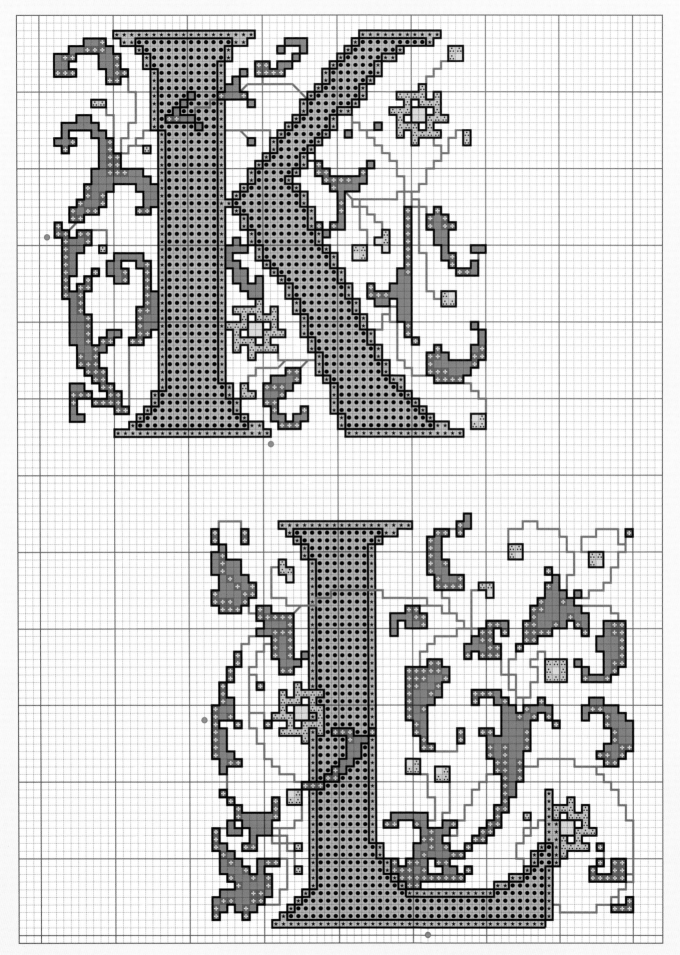

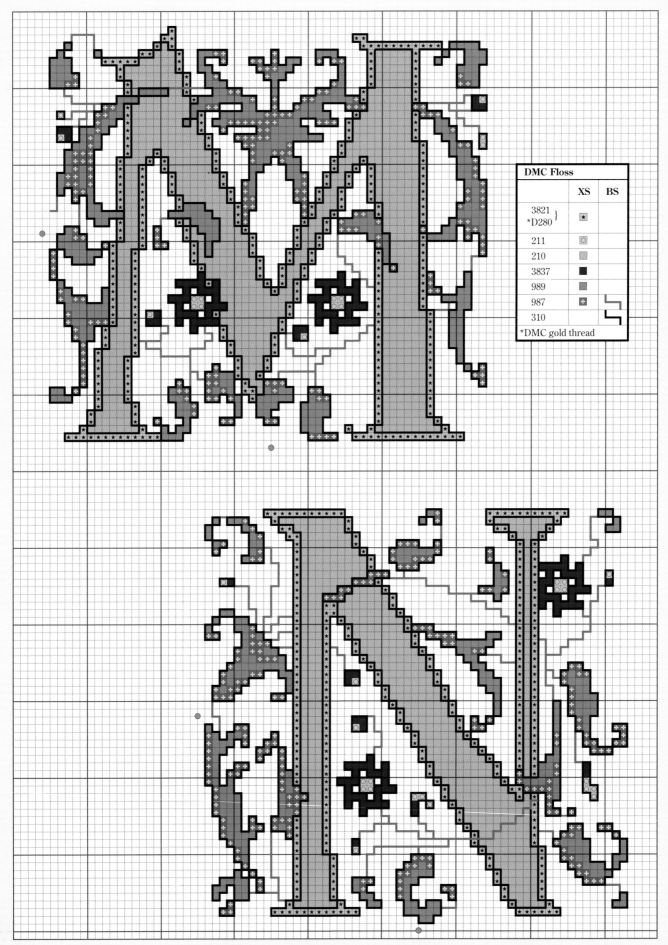

DMC Floss		
	XS	BS
3821 } *D280	★	
211	◎	
210	▨	
3837	■	
989	▨	
987	✚	
310		
*DMC gold thread		

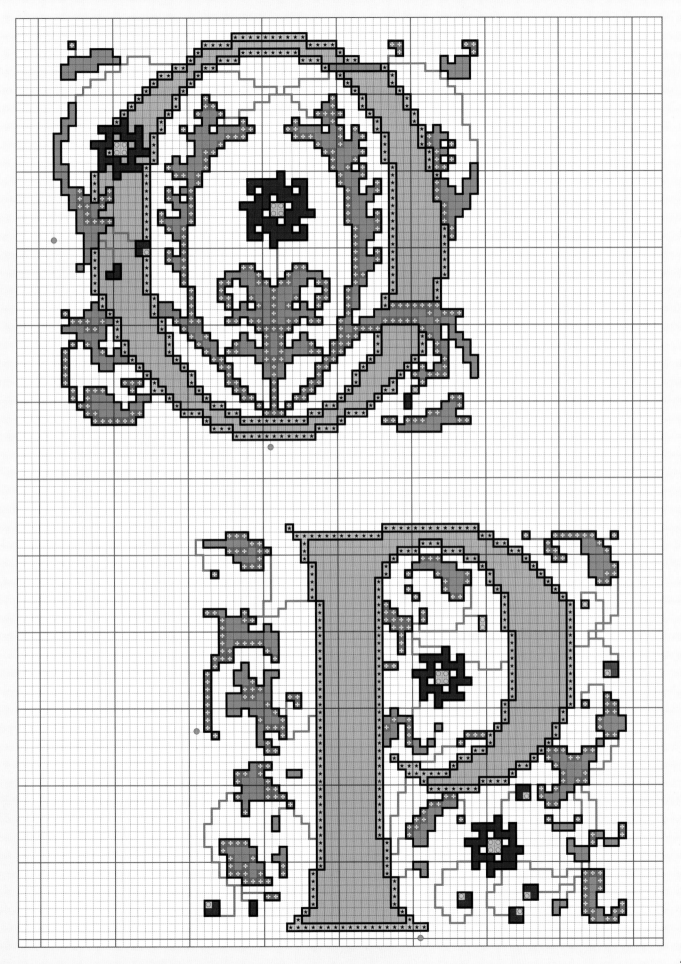

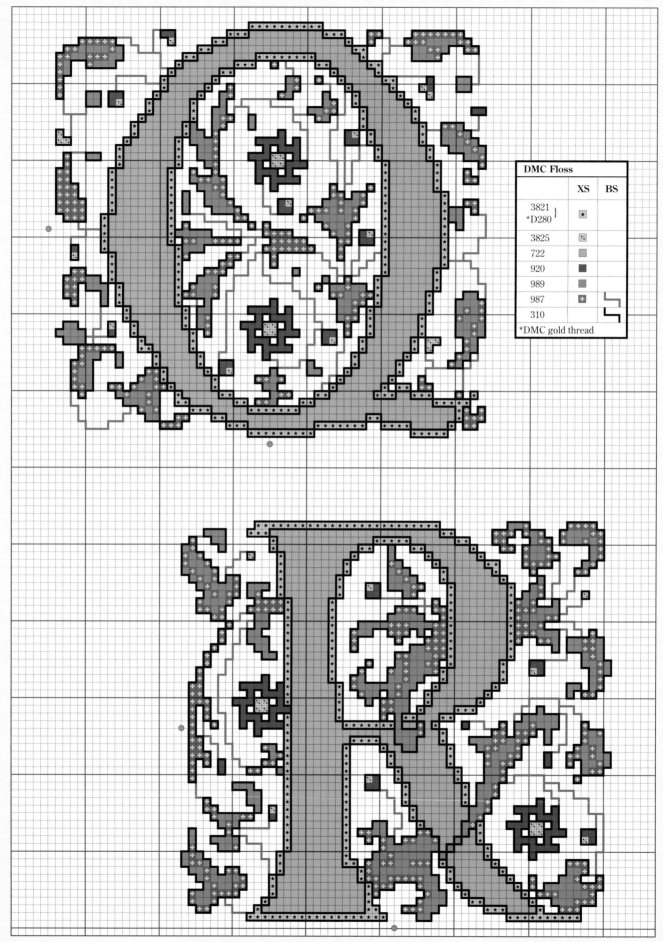

DMC Floss		
	XS	BS
3821 } *D280	★	
3825	▨	
722	▦	
920	◼	
989	◼	
987	✛	
310		
*DMC gold thread		

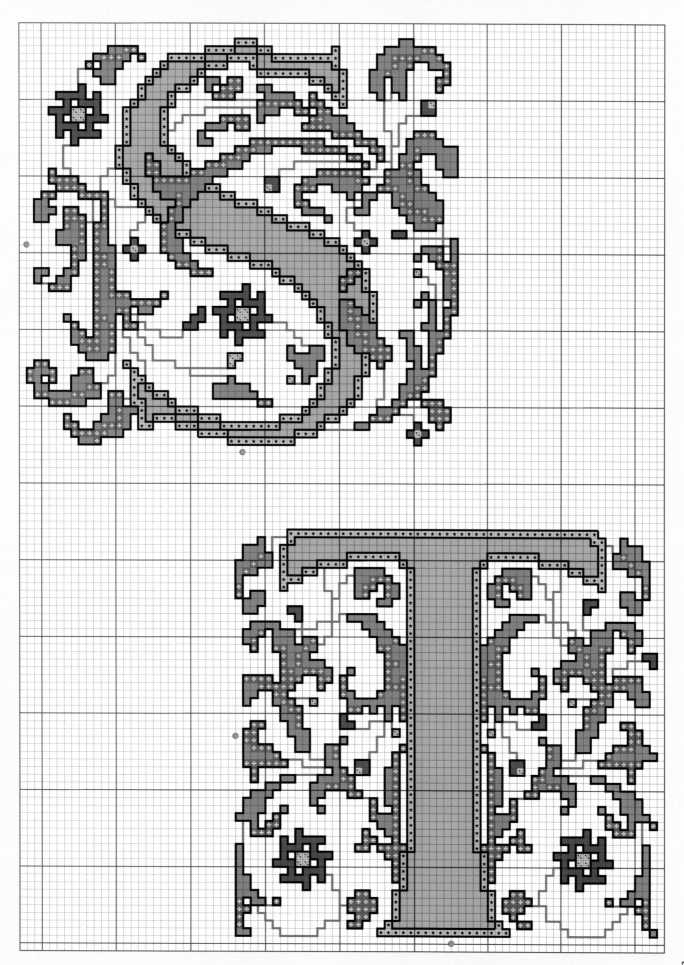

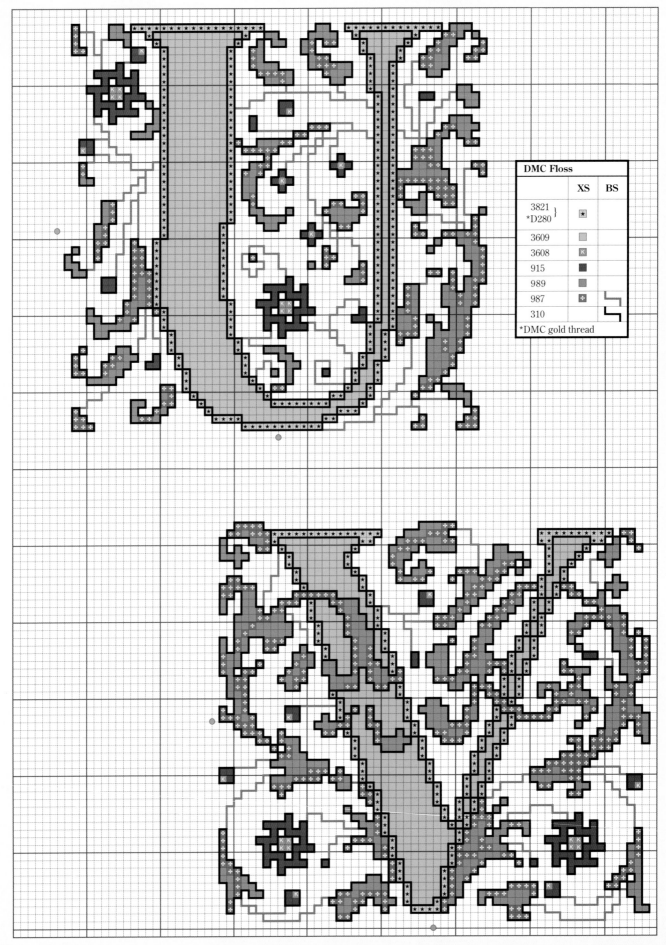

DMC Floss		
	XS	BS
3821 \} *D280	★	
3609		
3608	K	
915		
989		
987	✛	
310		
*DMC gold thread		

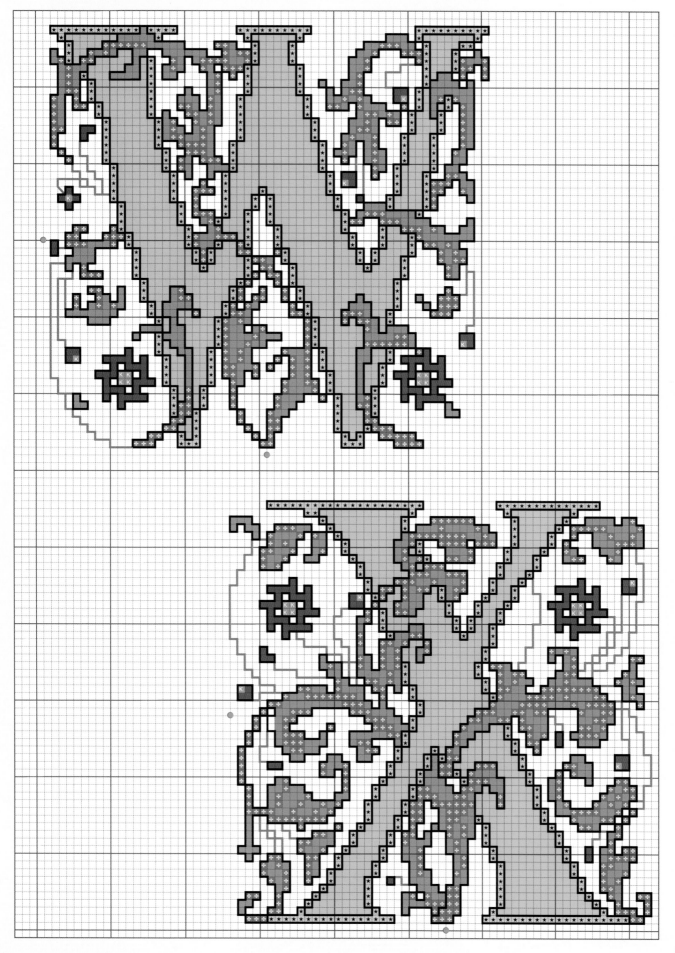

53

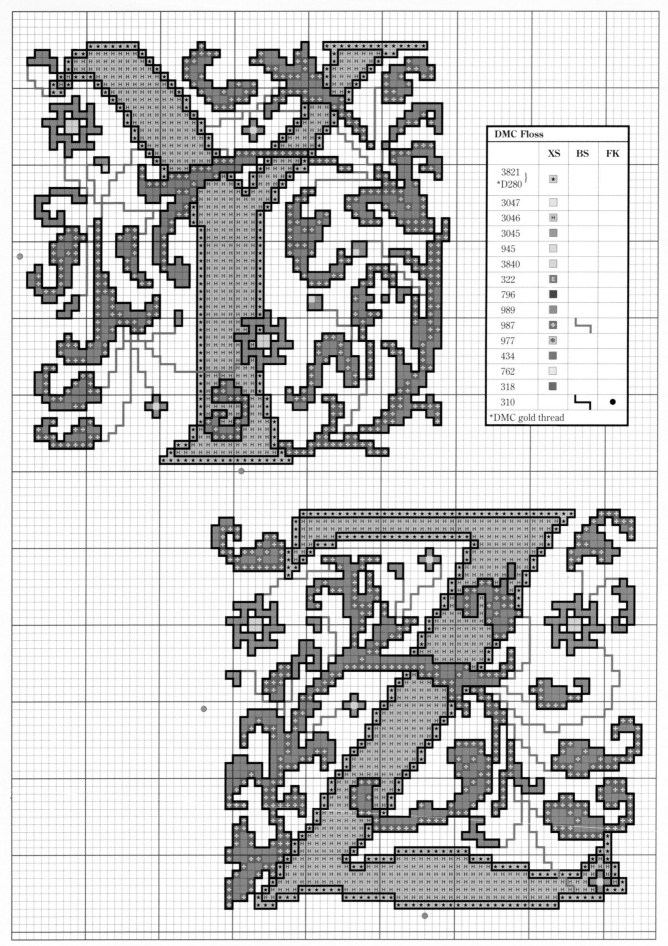

DMC Floss			
	XS	BS	FK
3821 } *D280	★		
3047			
3046	H		
3045			
945			
3840			
322	E		
796			
989			
987	✚	⌐	
977	❋		
434			
762			
318			
310		⌐	●
*DMC gold thread			

Catalina Floral

Motifs designed to be
stitched on lt. yellow fabric.

DMC Floss		
	XS	**BS**
744		
725		
3765		
320		
3814		
3777		
310		

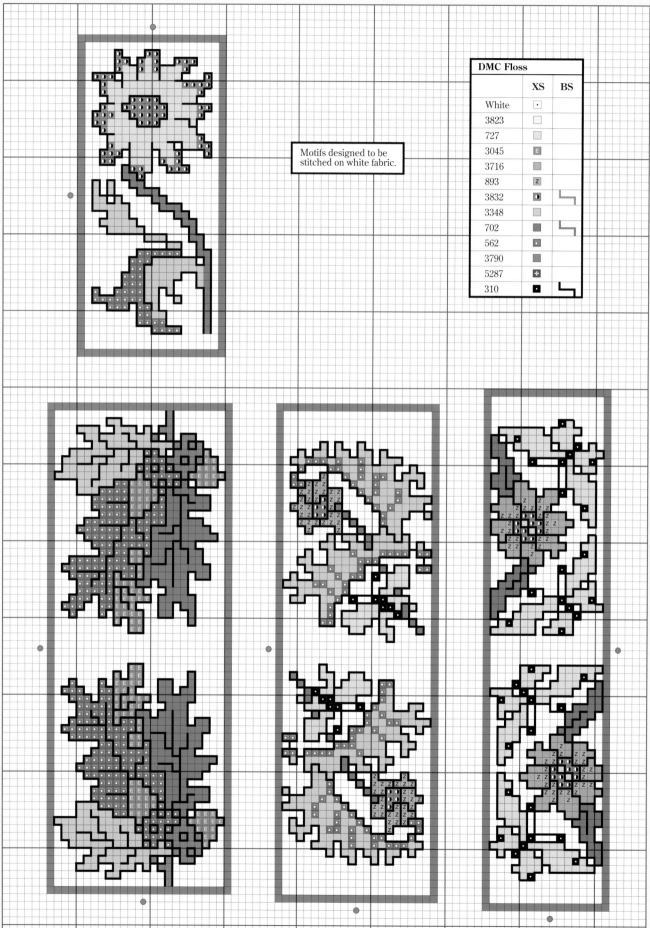

Motifs designed to be stitched on white fabric.

DMC Floss		
	XS	**BS**
White	⊡	
3823	☐	
727	☐	
3045	E	
3716	☐	
893	z	
3832	◖	⌐
3348	☐	
702	☐	⌐
562	⊡	
3790	☐	
5287	✦	
310	■	⌐

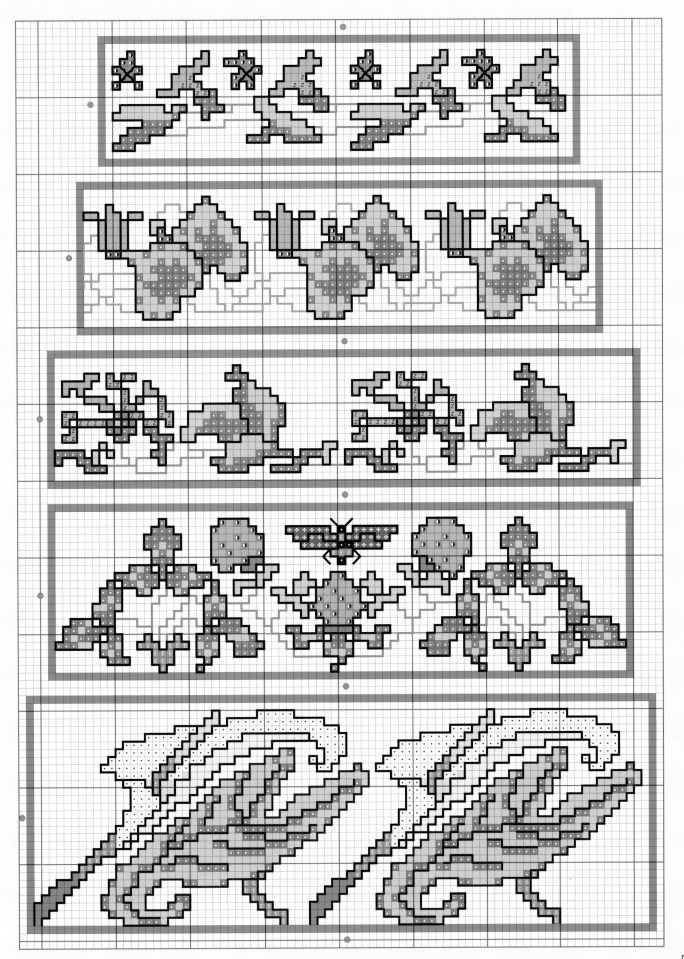

59

Motifs designed to be stitched on beige fabric.

DMC Floss	XS	BS
3078		
743		
3820		
221		
3835		
550		
988		
3345		
3371		

61

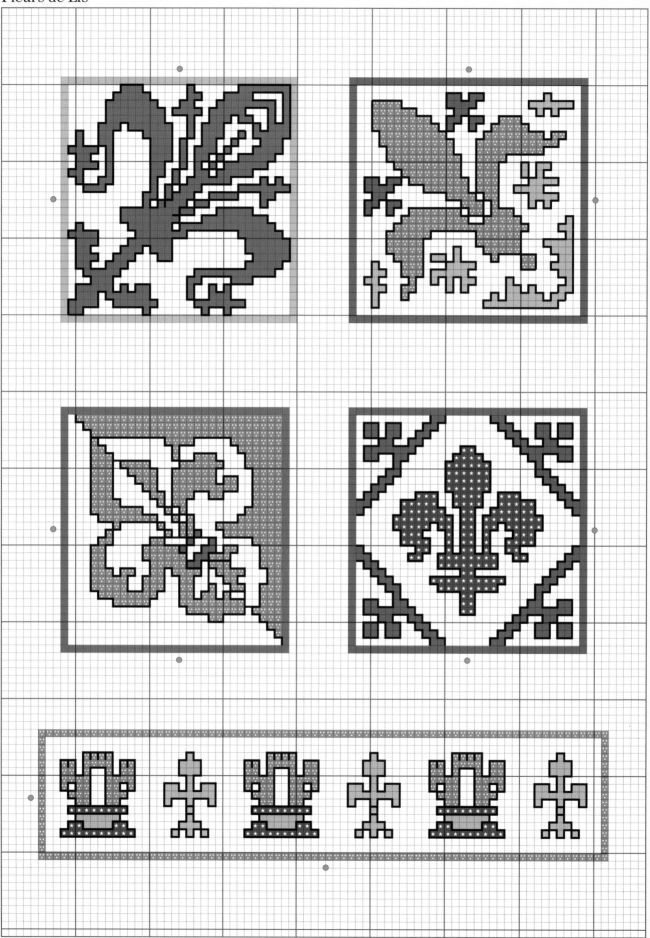

Motifs designed to be stitched on black fabric.

DMC Floss		
	XS	BS
3820		
782		
498		
921		
918		
840		
310		

Birds
of a
Feather

Motifs designed to be stitched on cream fabric.

DMC Floss	XS	BS
725		
327		
550		
809		
996		
820		
3766		
3812		
3814		
3815		
907		
3052		
700		
356		
415		
310		

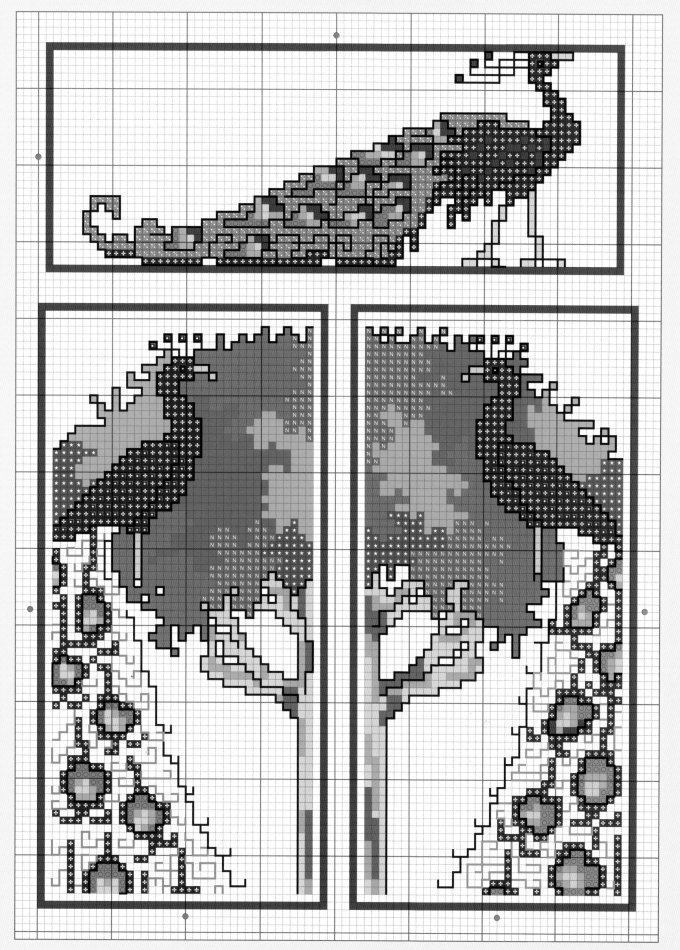

Barnyard

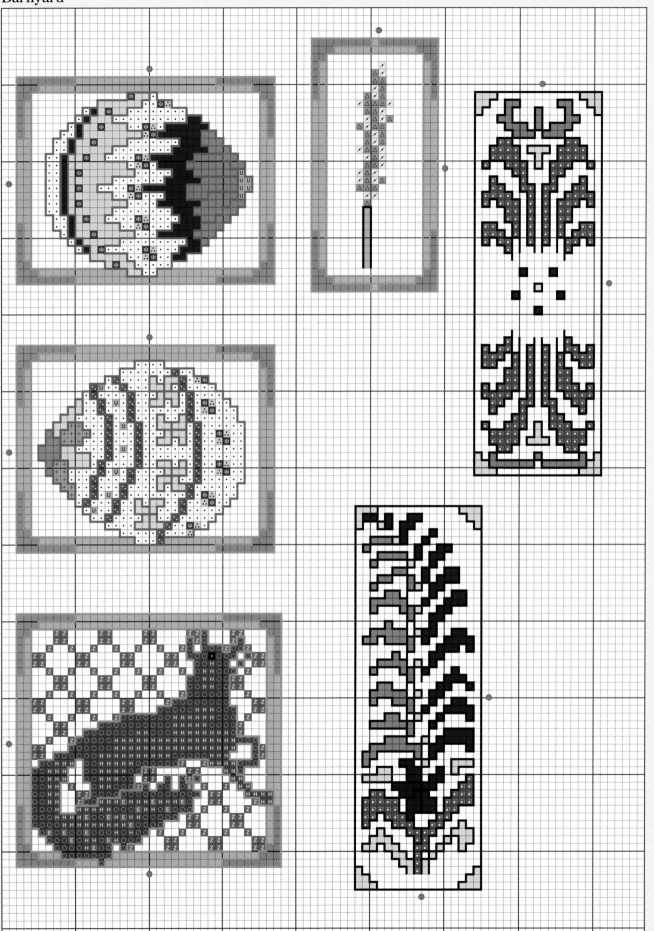

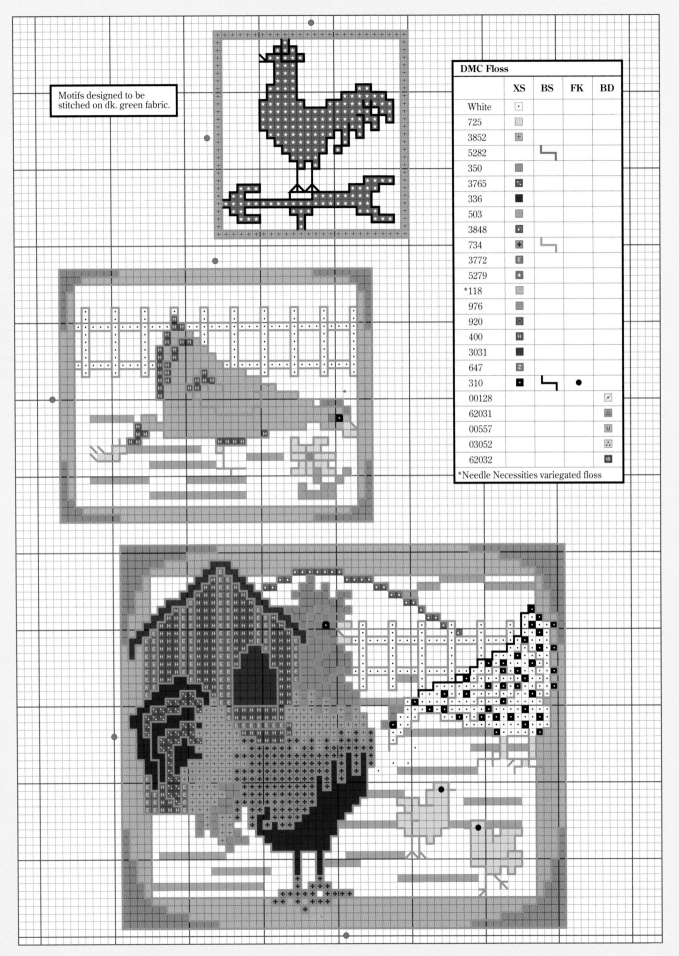

Motifs designed to be stitched on dk. green fabric.

DMC Floss				
	XS	**BS**	**FK**	**BD**
White	·			
725				
3852	+			
5282		⌐		
350				
3765	▨			
336	■			
503				
3848	⊡			
734	⊞	⌐		
3772	E			
5279	✶			
*118				
976				
920	◉			
400	H			
3031	■			
647	Z			
310	■	⌐	●	
00128				◹
62031				△
00557				U
03052				⊡
62032				❋

*Needle Necessities variegated floss

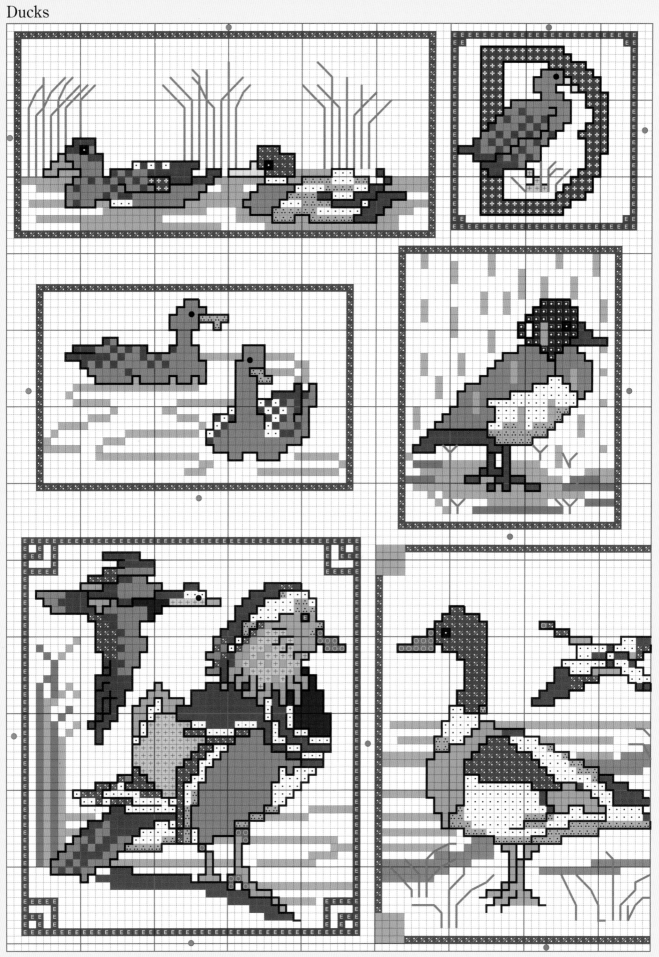

Motifs designed to be
stitched on lt. green fabric.

DMC Floss		DMC Floss		DMC Floss				DMC Floss			
	XS		XS		XS	BS	FK		XS	BS	FK
White	·	900	◎	792	✚			841	▨		
726	▫	3834	■	906	▪	⌐		3021	■		
3854	+	550	◪	890	⦂			415	⦂		
922	▨	932	▨	3808	E	⌐	●	310	▣	⌐	●

71

Motifs designed to be
stitched on lt. blue fabric.

DMC Floss		DMC Floss				DMC Floss		DMC Floss		
	XS		XS	BS	FK		XS		XS	BD
White	·	939		⌐	●	3816	◖	319	◨	
721	▥	927	z			993	⊠	5283	▢	
322	◉	704	▨			3850	▦	310	▪	
820	■	699	✚			320	N	02021		E

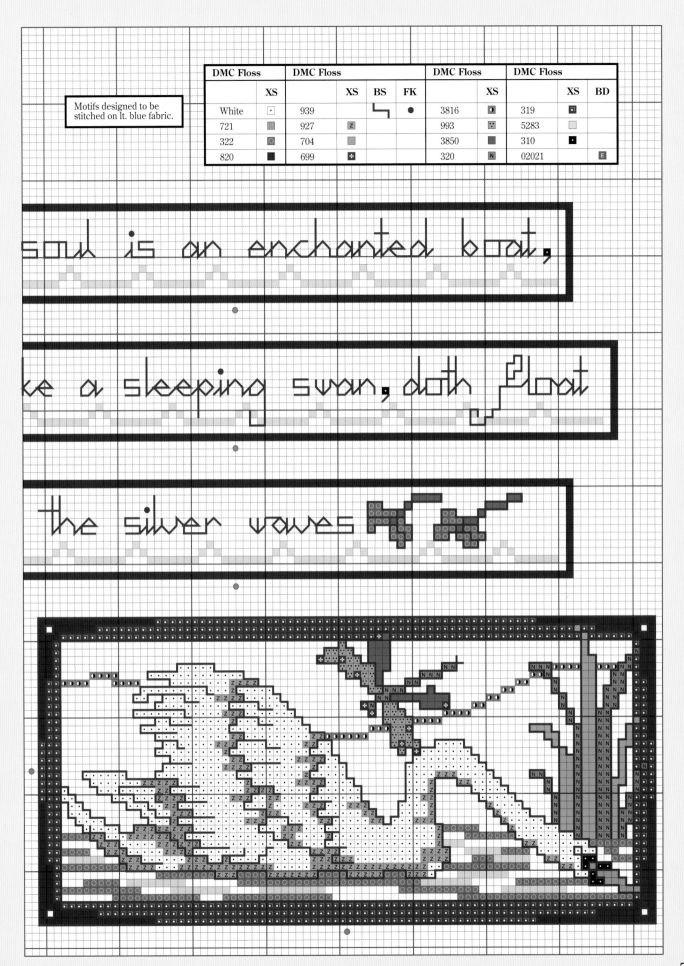

soul is an enchanted boat,

ke a sleeping swan, doth float

the silver waves

Motifs designed to be stitched on lt. blue fabric.

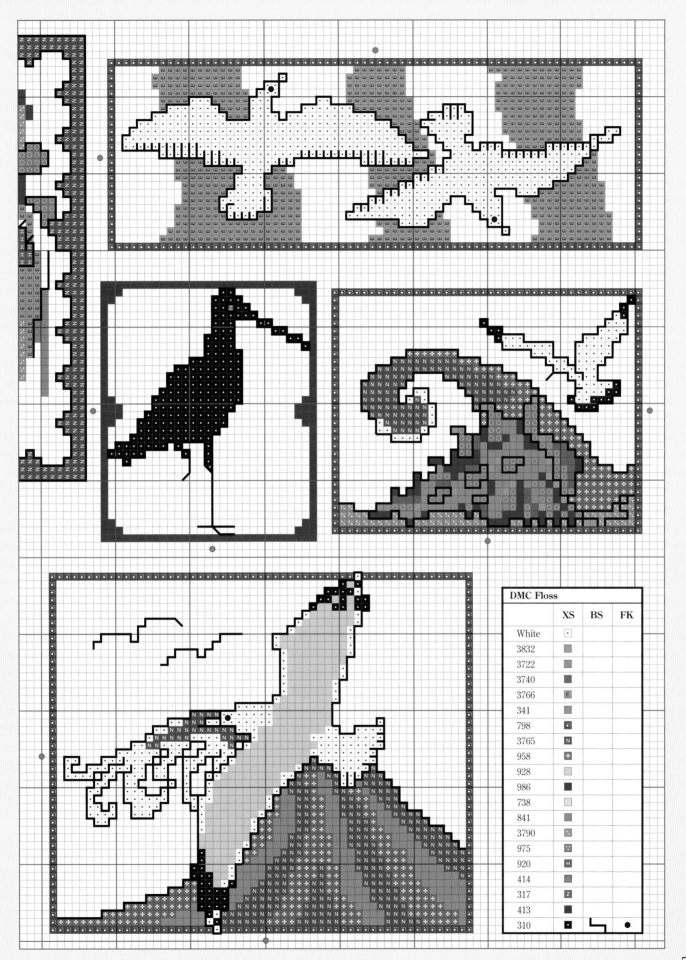

DMC Floss			
	XS	BS	FK
White	·		
3832			
3722	◎		
3740			
3766	E		
341			
798	▫		
3765	N		
958	✛		
928			
986			
738			
841			
3790	▨		
975	▣		
920	H		
414	△		
317	Z		
413			
310	▪	⌐	●

Motifs designed to be stitched on ivory fabric.

DMC Floss	XS	BS	BD
712	□		
3078	□		
726	△		
3820	▦		
957	▦		
3731	E		
321	▦		
498	▦		
798	▦		
824	▦		
904	▦	⌐	
988	▦		
986	◙		
950	▦		
3064	◎		
420	✚		
318	▦		
310	■	L	
02012			✚
00525			▦
02014			H

77

Motifs designed to be
stitched on black fabric.

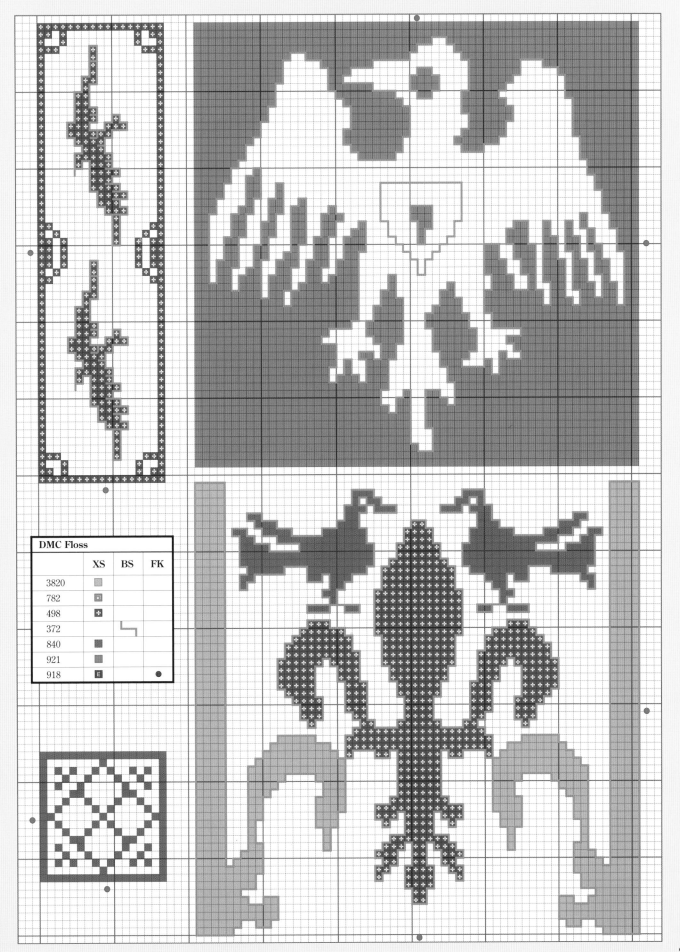

DMC Floss

	XS	BS	FK
3820			
782			
498			
372			
840			
921			
918	E		●

Simple Geometrics

Heart Geometric

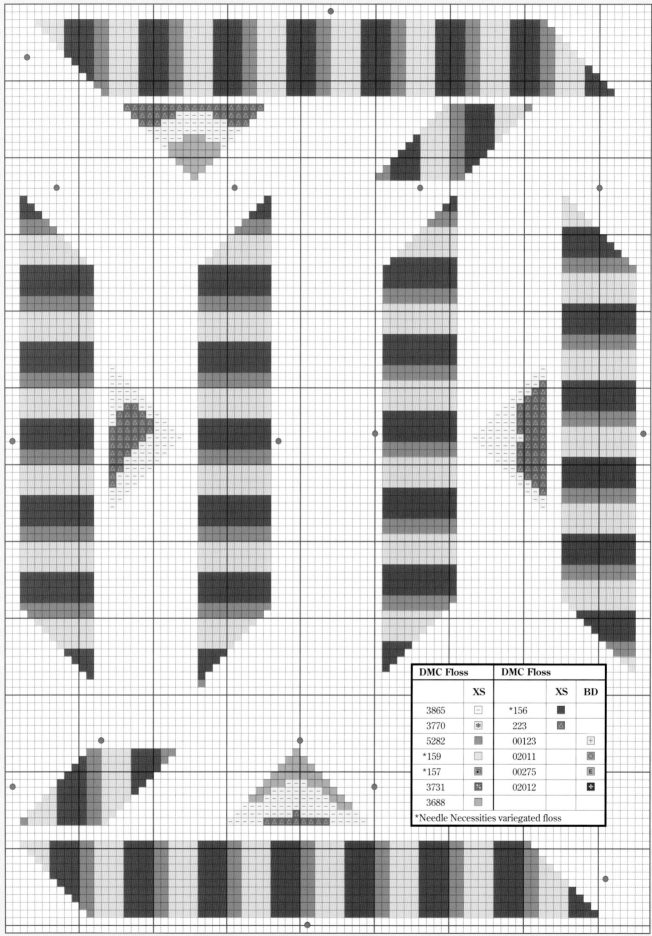

DMC Floss		DMC Floss		
	XS		**XS**	**BD**
3865	⊟	*156	■	
3770	✳	223	▲	
5282	▨	00123		⊞
*159	☐	02011		◉
*157	▣	00275		E
3731	▨	02012		✦
3688	▨			
*Needle Necessities variegated floss				

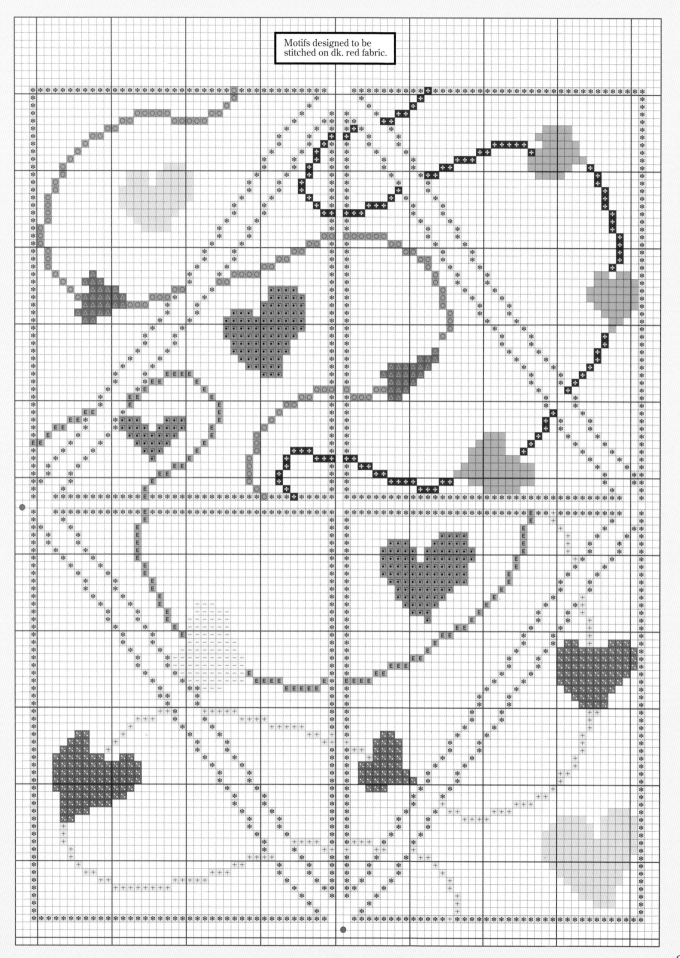

Motifs designed to be
stitched on dk. red fabric.

83

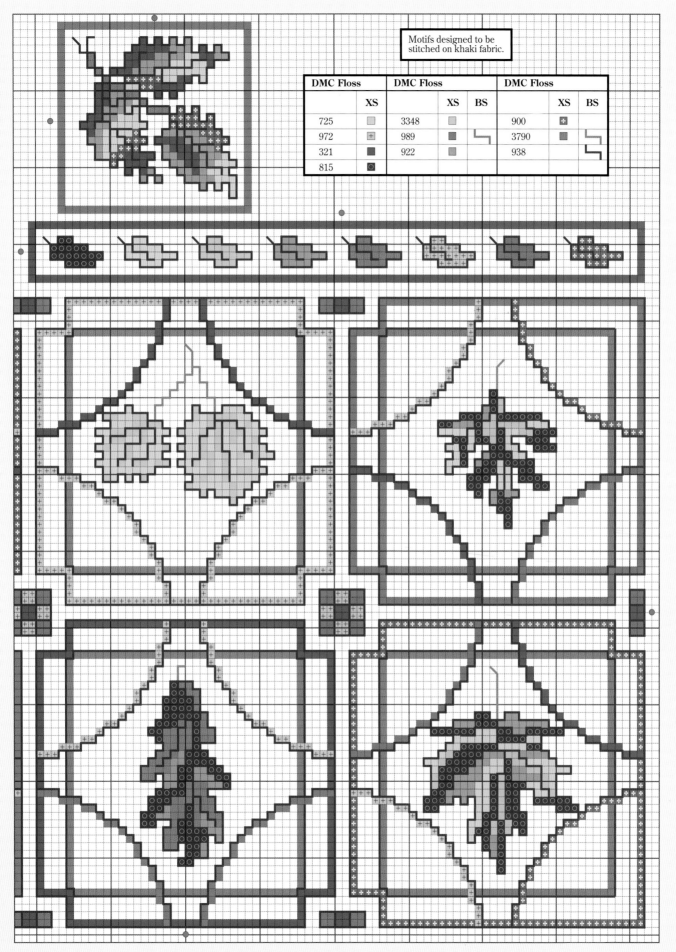

Motifs designed to be
stitched on khaki fabric.

DMC Floss			DMC Floss			DMC Floss		
	XS			XS	BS		XS	BS
725			3348			900		
972			989			3790		
321			922			938		
815								

Kazak Geometric

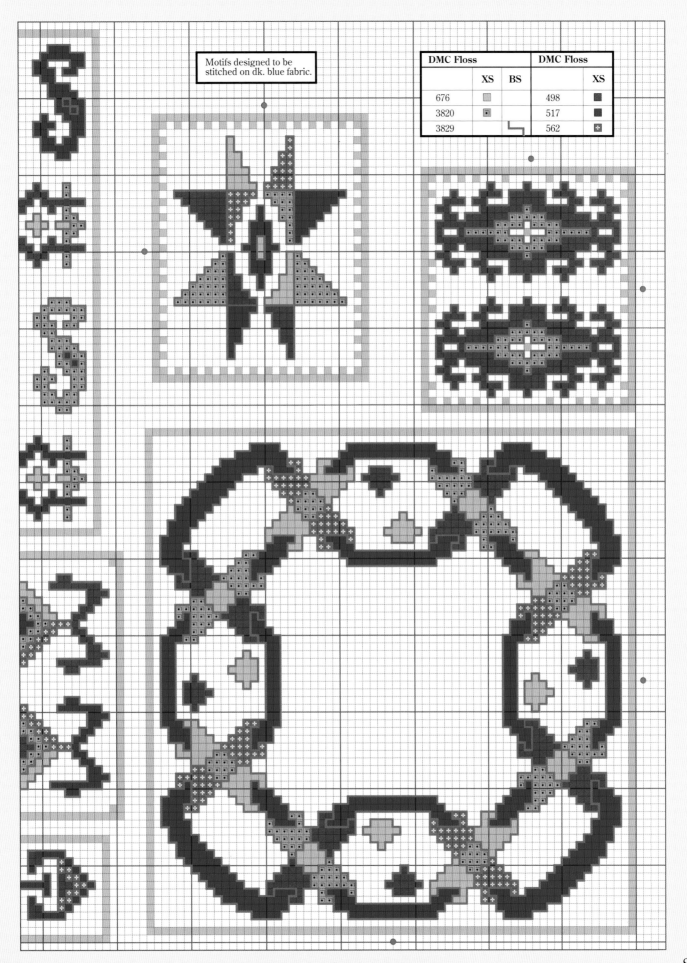

Motifs designed to be
stitched on dk. blue fabric.

DMC Floss			DMC Floss	
	XS	BS		XS
676			498	
3820			517	
3829			562	

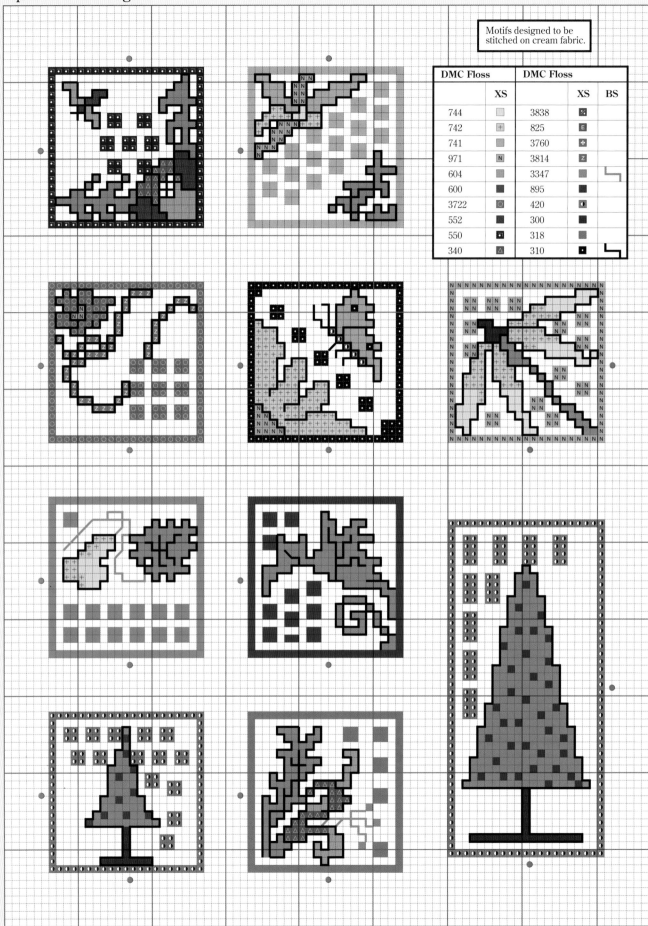

DMC Floss		DMC Floss		
	XS		XS	BS
744		3838		
742	+	825	E	
741		3760		
971	N	3814	Z	
604		3347		
600		895		
3722		420		
552		300		
550		318		
340		310		

Motifs designed to be stitched on cream fabric.

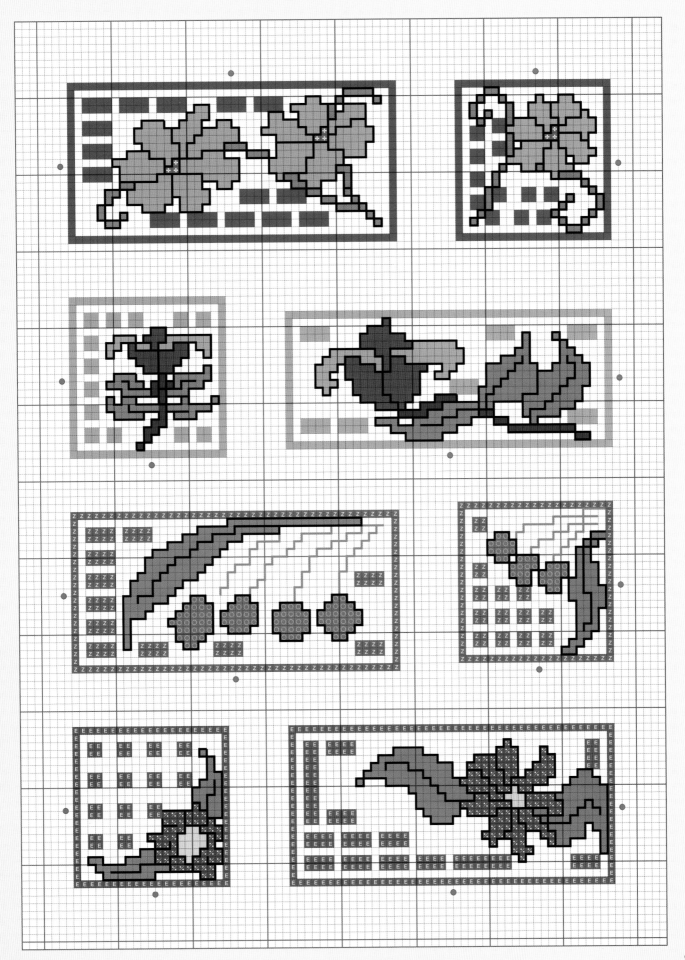

Triangles

DMC Floss		DMC Floss			DMC Floss			
	XS		XS	BS		XS	BS	BD
3078	▫	987	✠		317	▨		
726	⊞	935		⌐	5287		⌐	
742	▦	890	E		310	▪		
3766	▨	370	◎		02002			△
3809	▨	831	Z		00423			H
3052	▨	3021	★		02020			S
3051	▨	898	■		02010			◖
3348	▨							

Motifs designed to be stitched on yellow fabric.

90

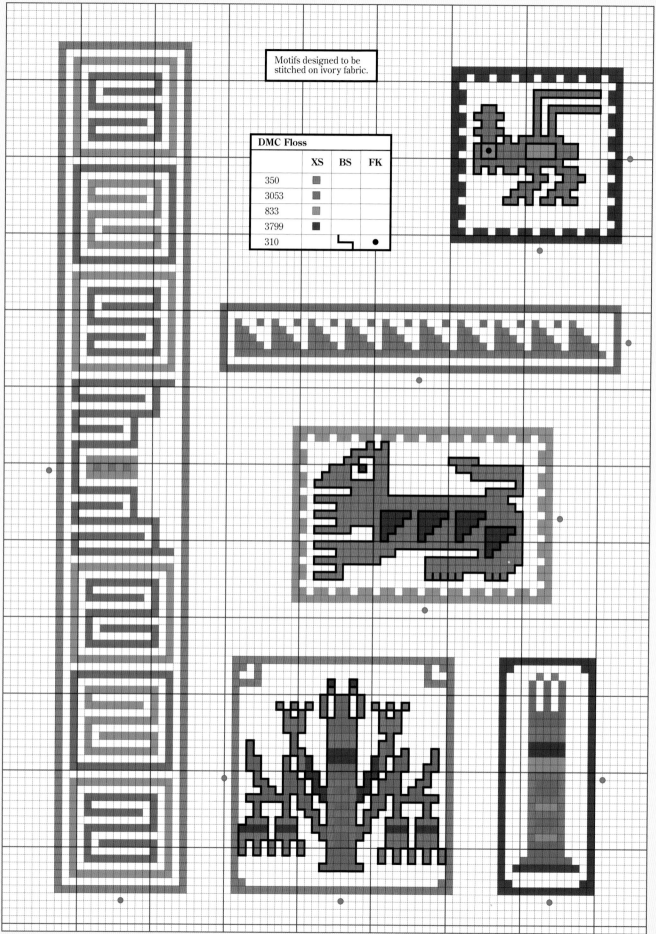

Motifs designed to be
stitched on ivory fabric.

DMC Floss			
	XS	BS	FK
350			
3053			
833			
3799			
310			●

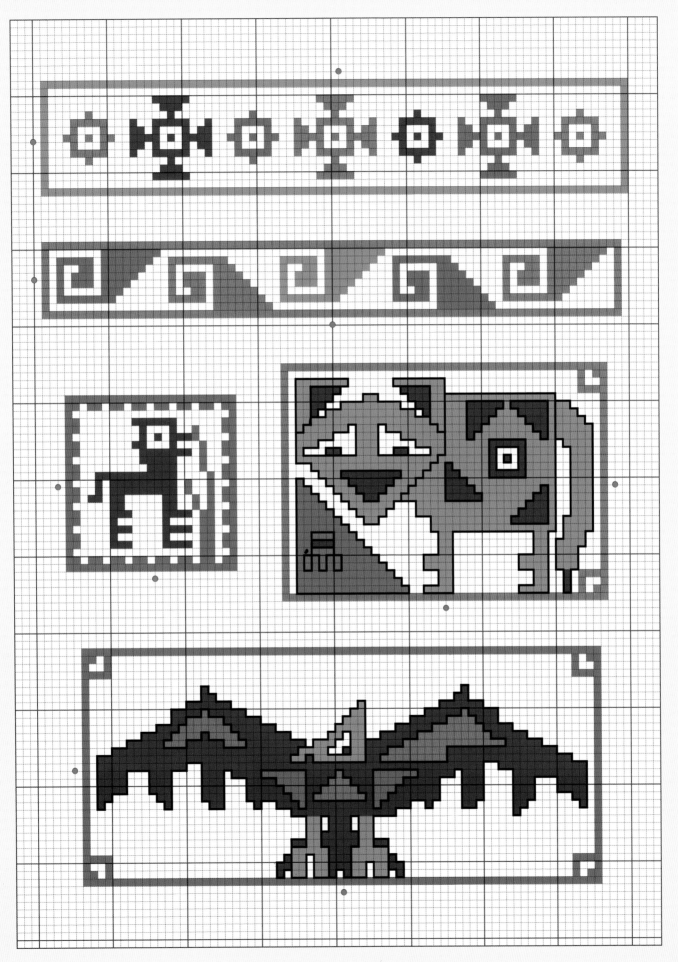

Outragious Paisley

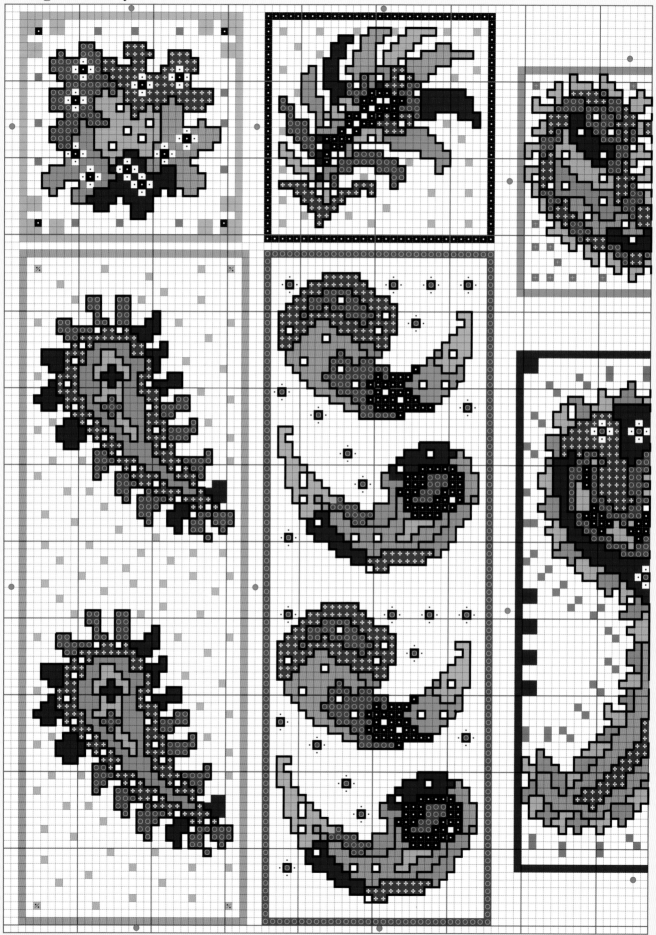

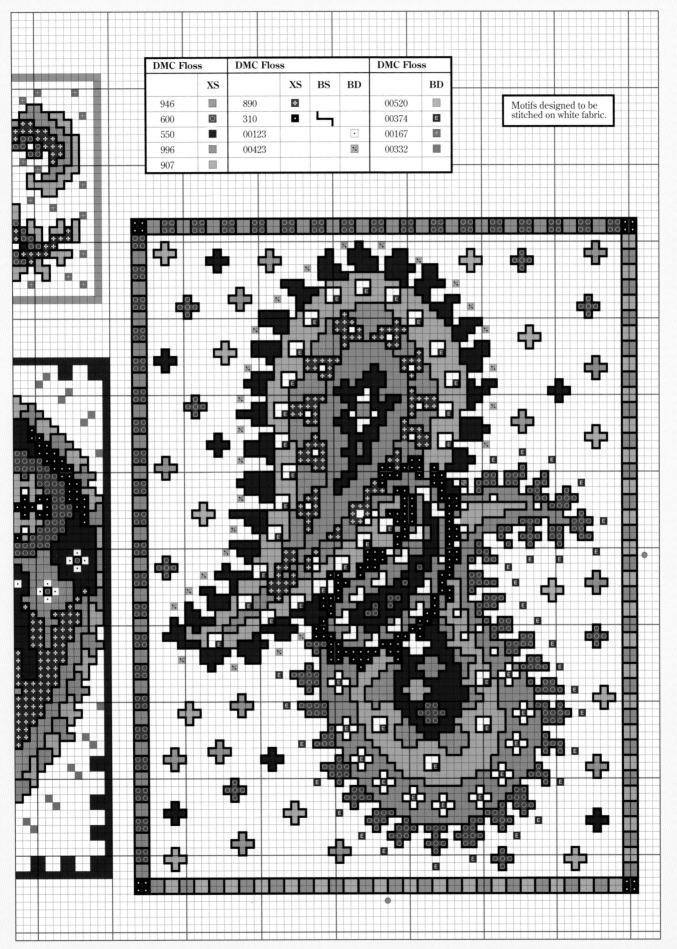

DMC Floss		DMC Floss				DMC Floss	
	XS		XS	BS	BD		BD
946		890				00520	
600		310				00374	E
550		00123			·	00167	
996		00423				00332	
907							

Motifs designed to be stitched on white fabric.

DMC Floss		
	XS	**BS**
782	▨	
930	▣	
355	◉	
434	▣	
840	▨	
844	✚	
310		

Motifs designed to be stitched on lt. mocha fabric.

Art Deco Stained Glass

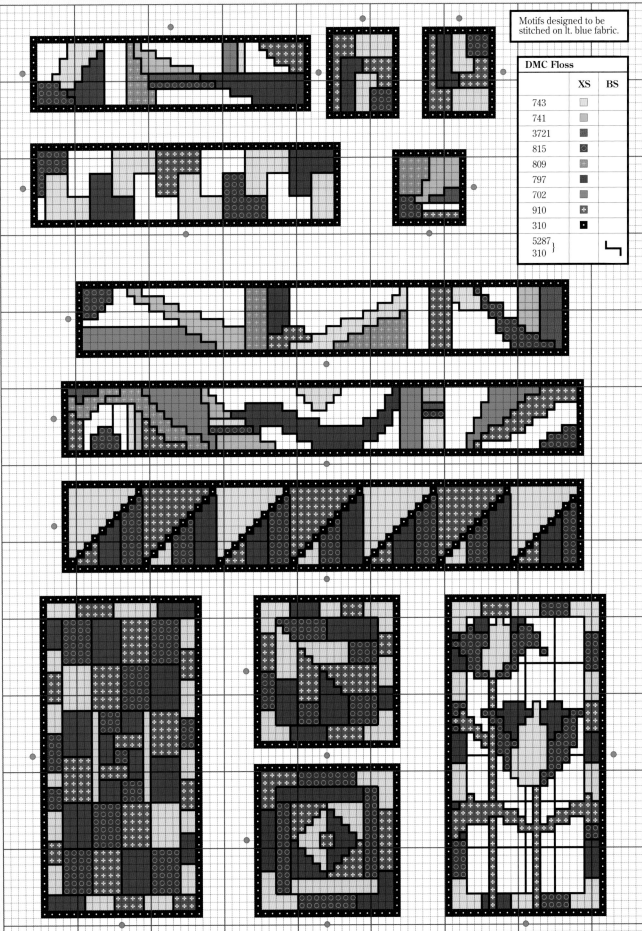

Motifs designed to be stitched on lt. blue fabric.

DMC Floss		
	XS	**BS**
743		
741		
3721		
815		
809		
797		
702		
910		
310		
5287 } 310		

It
Began
in a
Garden

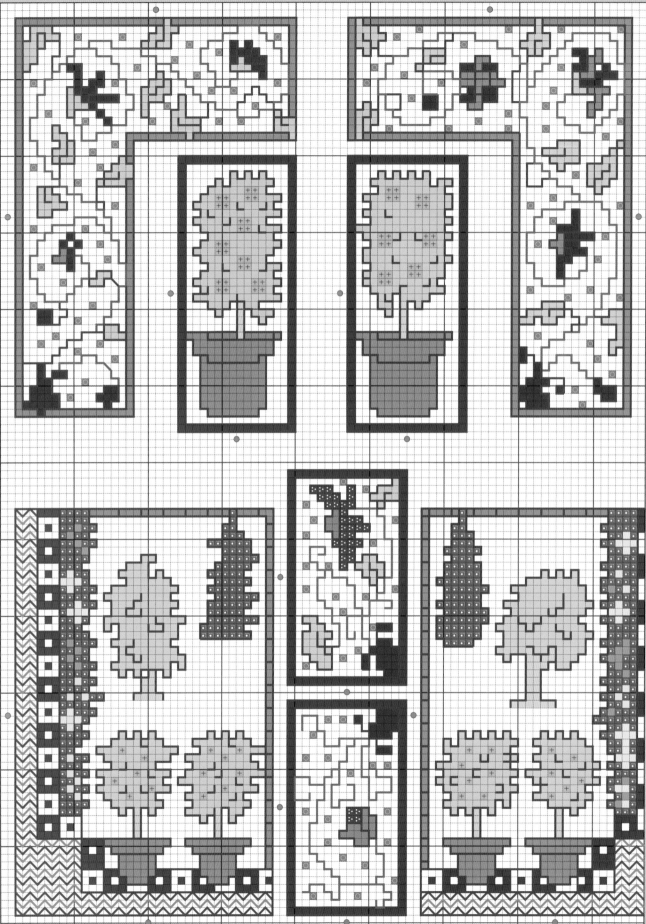

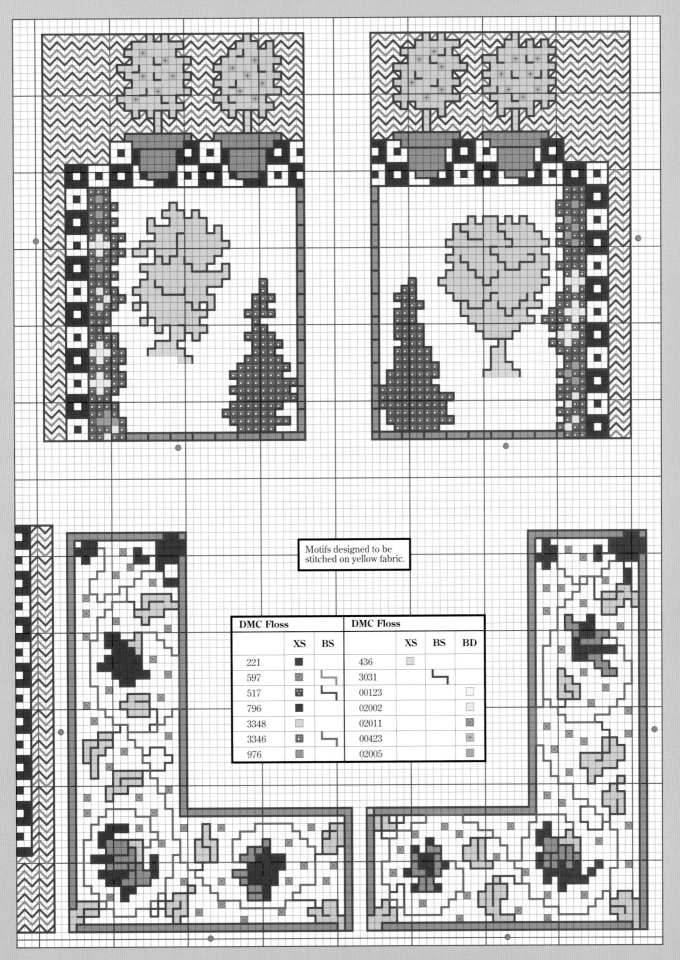

Motifs designed to be
stitched on yellow fabric.

DMC Floss			DMC Floss			
	XS	BS		XS	BS	BD
221	■		436	▢		
597	▨	⌐	3031		⌐	
517	▣	⌐	00123			▢
796	■		02002			▢
3348	▨		02011			◉
3346	▣	⌐	00423			+
976	▨		02005			▨

Motifs designed to be
stitched on med. green fabric.

DMC Floss

	XS	BS
White	·	
743		
972		
3689		
3350		⌐
349	○	
340		
3746		
799		
939		⌐
3346		
986	N	⌐
3776		
3826	E	
5279		
738		
436		
434	△	⌐
3072		

Motifs designed to be
stitched on lt. mocha fabric.

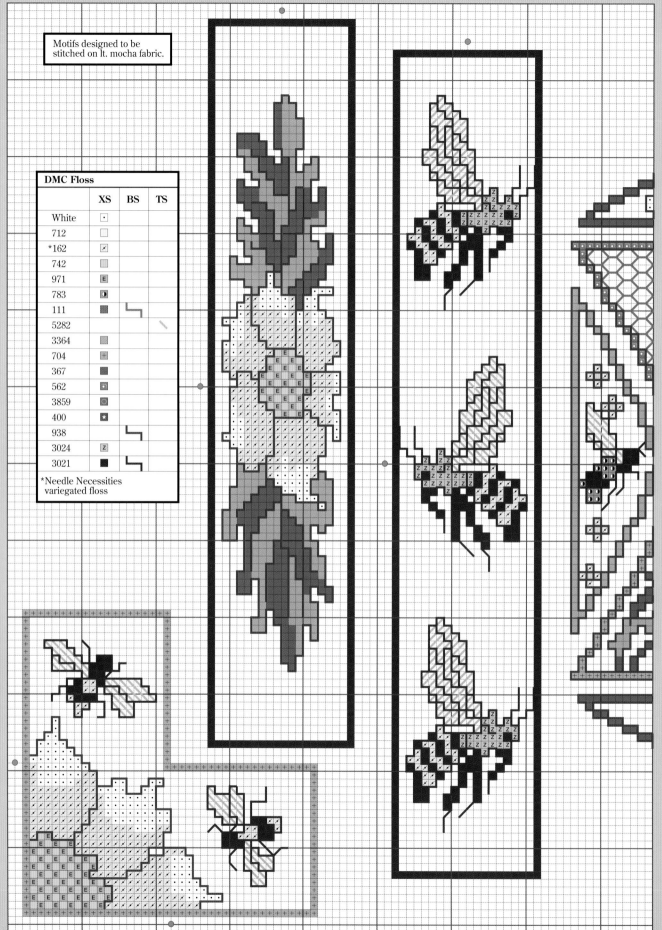

DMC Floss			
	XS	BS	TS
White	·		
712			
*162	⟋		
742			
971	E		
783	◑		
111		⌐	
5282			
3364			
704	+		
367			
562	▣		
3859	◉		
400	★		
938		⌐	
3024	z		
3021	■	⌐	

*Needle Necessities
variegated floss

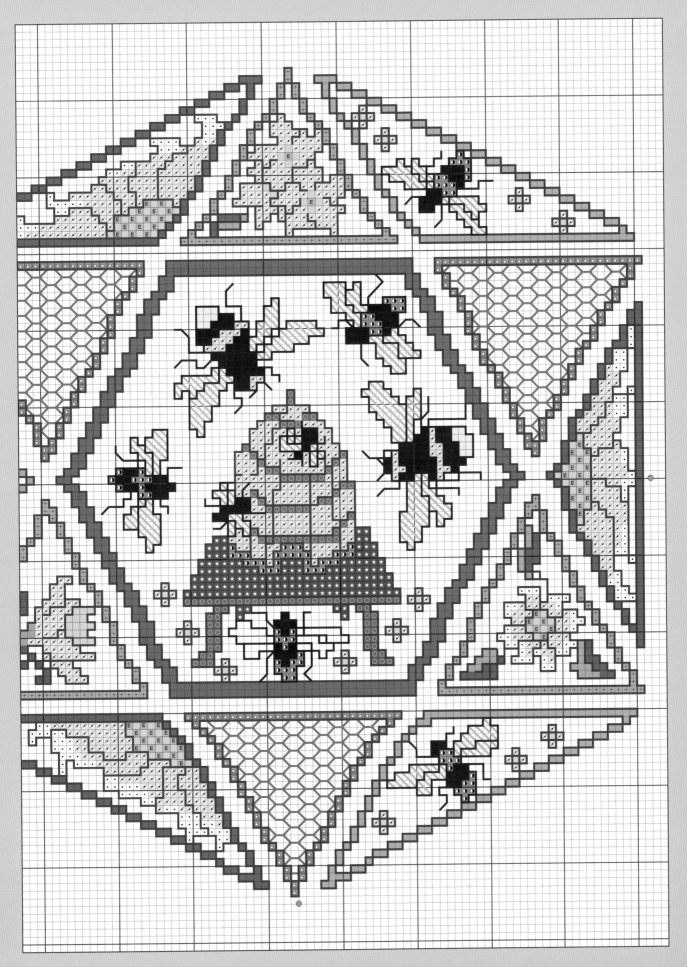

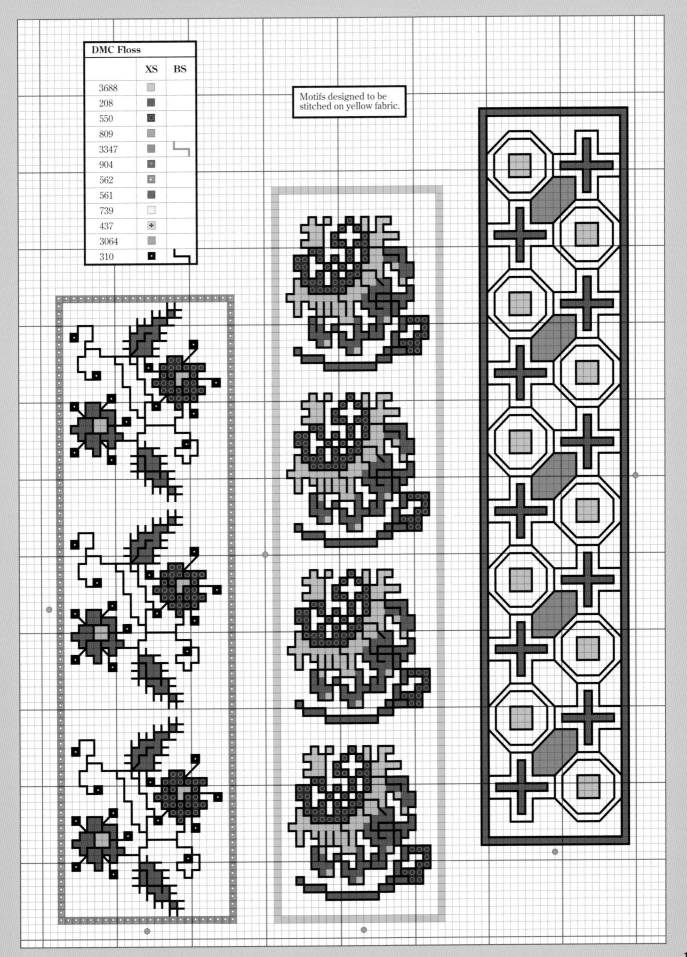

DMC Floss		
	XS	BS
3688		
208		
550		
809		
3347		
904		
562		
561		
739		
437		
3064		
310		

Motifs designed to be stitched on yellow fabric.

Knot Garden

DMC Floss		DMC Floss			DMC Floss			DMC Floss		DMC Floss	
	XS		XS	BS		XS	BS		BD		BD
102	■	986	■		69	◙		02010	⊟	03019	▦
67	▨	502	▲		920	■		02002	◪	03020	S
92	■	501	U	⌐	844			02011	⠇	03023	✳
*142	✚	500	E		318	■		00145	▢	02007	K
936	▣	738		⌐	5287	✚		02004	H	03061	★
701	▨	105	▨		3799	N		00151	Z	02008	◈
988	◉										

*Needle Necessities variegated floss

Motifs designed to be
stitched on lt. green fabric.

110

Study in Color

Hearts of Gold

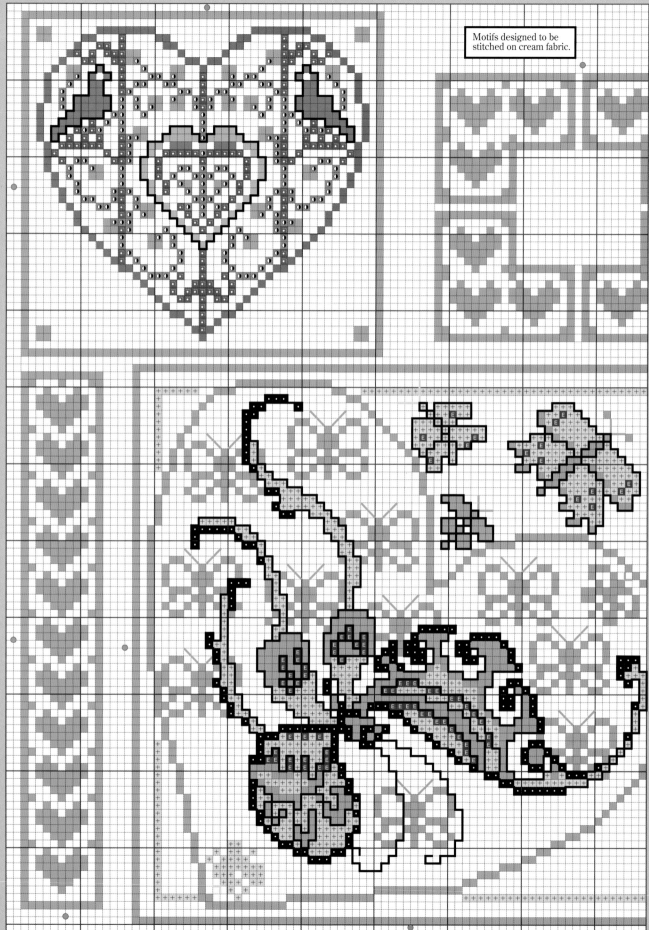

Motifs designed to be
stitched on cream fabric.

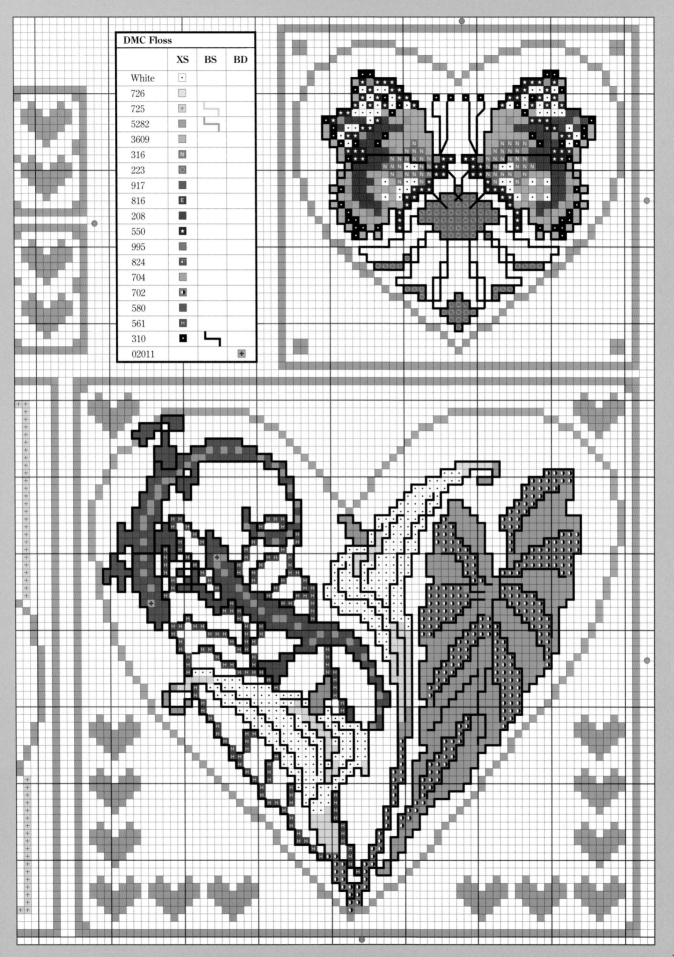

DMC Floss			
	XS	BS	BD
White	·		
726			
725	+		
5282			
3609			
316	N		
223	◎		
917			
816	E		
208			
550	✶		
995			
824	▣		
704			
702	◑		
580			
561	H		
310	■		
02011			✛

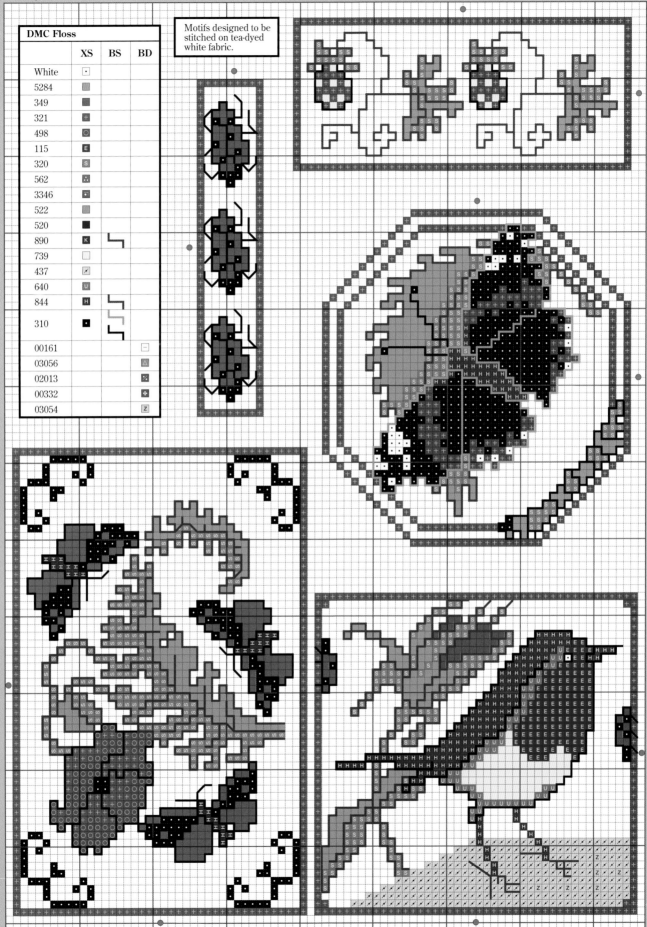

DMC Floss			
	XS	**BS**	**BD**
White	·		
5284			
349			
321	+		
498	◌		
115	E		
320	S		
562	⦂		
3346	▫		
522			
520			
890	K	⌐	
739	▫		
437	◿		
640	U		
844	H	⌐	
310	■	⌐	
00161			⊟
03056			△
02013			⊠
00332			⊞
03054			Z

Motifs designed to be stitched on tea-dyed white fabric.

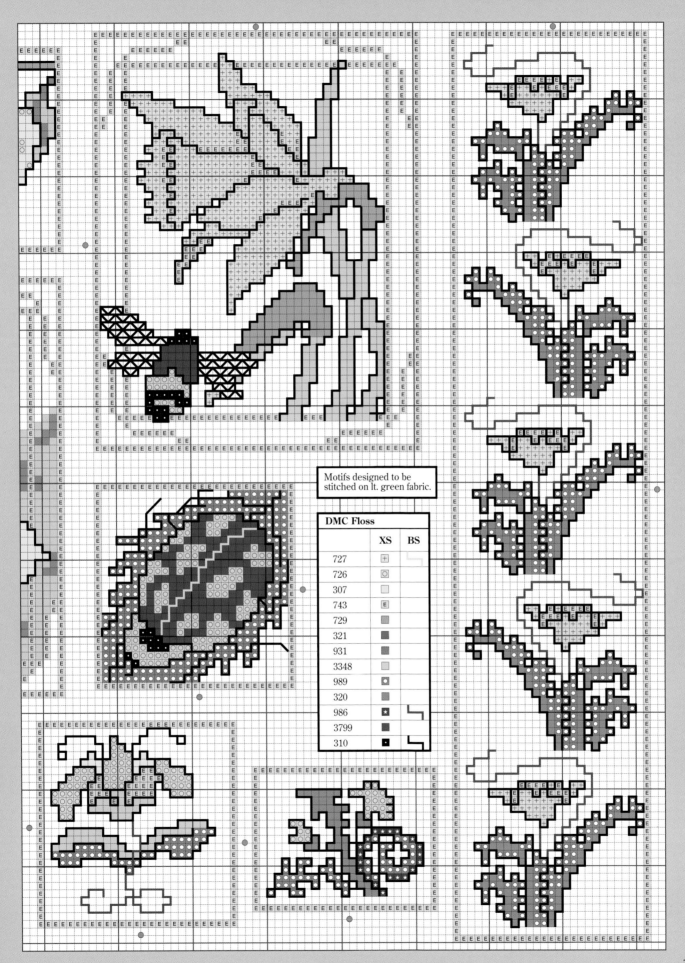

Motifs designed to be
stitched on lt. green fabric.

DMC Floss		
	XS	**BS**
727	+	
726	◎	
307	☐	
743	E	
729	▨	
321	▨	
931	▨	
3348	☐	
989	◉	
320	▨	
986	✦	
3799	▨	
310	▪	

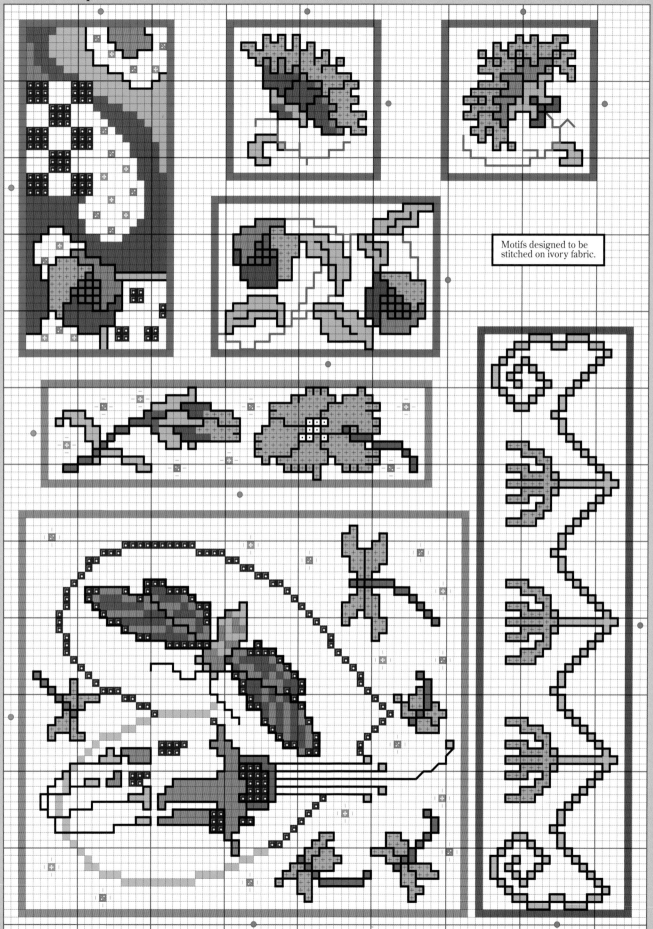

Motifs designed to be
stitched on ivory fabric.

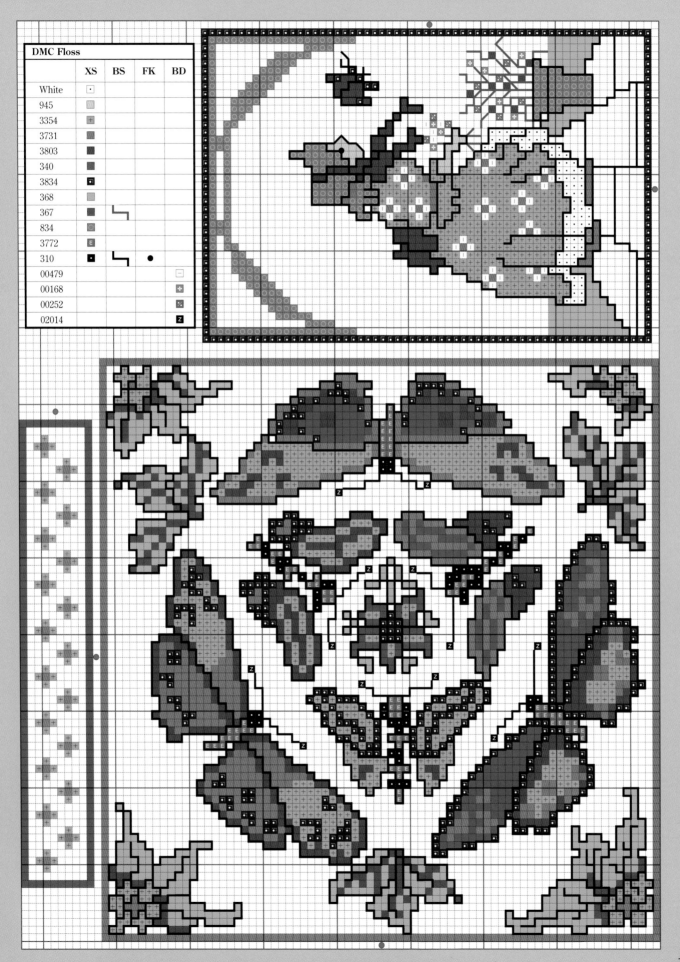

DMC Floss				
	XS	BS	FK	BD
White	·			
945				
3354	+			
3731				
3803				
340				
3834	▣			
368				
367		⌐		
834				
3772	E			
310	■	⌐	●	
00479				⊡
00168				✦
00252				✶
02014				Z

121

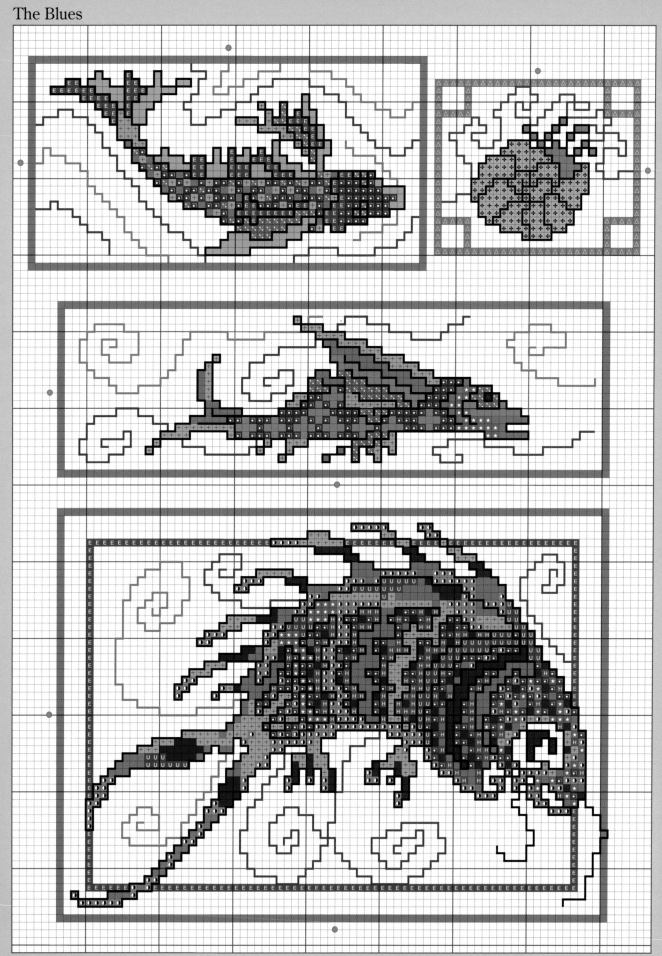

DMC Floss			
	XS	BS	BD
321	■		
340	▨		
333	■		
798	U		
797	▣		
312	◎		
519	✛		
517	E		
5290		⌐	
5291		⌐	
807	■		
3765	H		
597	◑		
959	▨		
704	+		
3347	▨		
3815	✦	⌐	
310	▪	⌐	
00128			▨
00252			△

Motifs designed to be stitched on lt. blue fabric.

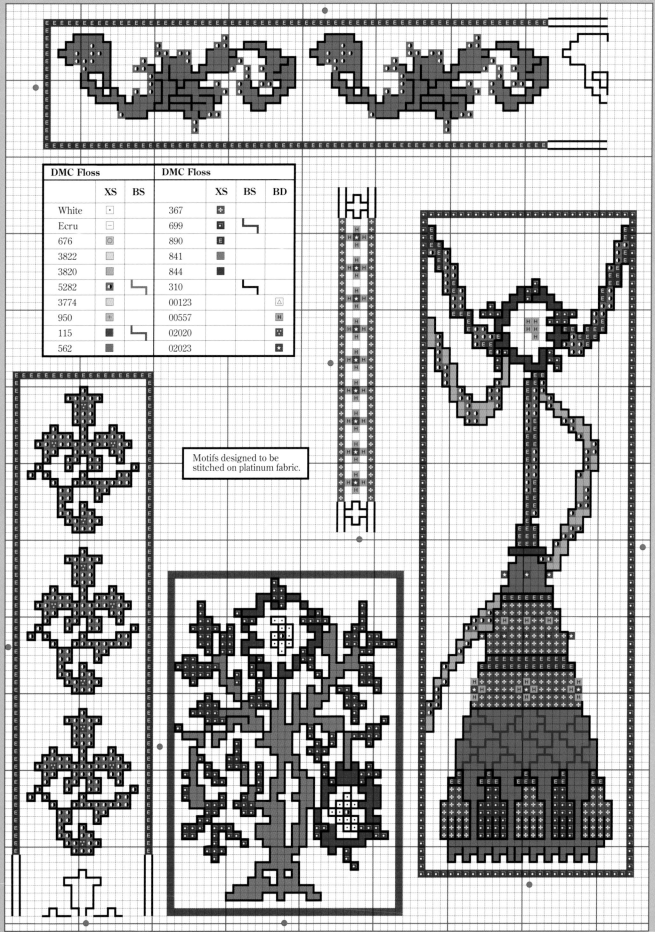

DMC Floss			DMC Floss			
	XS	BS		XS	BS	BD
White	·		367	+		
Ecru	−		699	▫	⌐	
676	◎		890	E		
3822	▨		841	▦		
3820	▨		844	■		
5282	◑	⌐	310		⌐	
3774	▨		00123			△
950	+		00557			H
115	■	⌐	02020			▨
562	■		02023			★

Motifs designed to be
stitched on platinum fabric.

Block Samples

Pages 26–27 Up in the Heavens

Pages 28–29 Along the Village Street

Pages 62–63 Fleurs-de-Lis

Pages 72–73 Swans

When the world wearies
And society ceases to satisfy
There is always the garden.

Pages 14–15 In the Garden

A church of silent weathered looks
A breezy reddish tower
A yard whose mounded resting nooks
Are tinged with sorrel flower

Pages 20–21 In a Country Churchyard

Pages 76–77 Hoopoe & Macaws

Pages 90–91 Triangles

Pages 102–103 Islamic Garden

Pages 108–109 Formal Garden

127

Metric Conversion Chart

mm-millimetres cm-centimetres
inches to millimetres and centimetres

inches	mm	cm	inches	cm	inches	cm
⅛	3	0.3	9	22.9	30	76.2
¼	6	0.6	10	25.4	31	78.7
⅜	10	1.0	11	27.9	32	81.3
½	13	1.3	12	30.5	33	83.8
⅝	16	1.6	13	33.0	34	86.4
¾	19	1.9	14	35.6	35	88.9
⅞	22	2.2	15	38.1	36	91.4
1	25	2.5	16	40.6	37	94.0
1¼	32	3.2	17	43.2	38	96.5
1½	38	3.8	18	45.7	39	99.1
1¾	44	4.4	19	48.3	40	101.6
2	51	5.1	20	50.8	41	104.1
2½	64	6.4	21	53.3	42	106.7
3	76	7.6	22	55.9	43	109.2
3½	89	8.9	23	58.4	44	111.8
4	102	10.2	24	61.0	45	114.3
4½	114	11.4	25	63.5	46	116.8
5	127	12.7	26	66.0	47	119.4
6	152	15.2	27	68.6	48	121.9
7	178	17.8	28	71.1	49	124.5
8	203	20.3	29	73.7	50	127.0

Index